THE TRANSCENDENT MIRROR
A Bicentennial Anthology for Deerfield

In memory of Frank L. Boyden and Helen C. Boyden, who taught us

THE TRANSCENDENT MIRROR
A Bicentennial Anthology for Deerfield

§

Janet W. B. Rogers
Eric Widmer

Editors

DEERFIELD ACADEMY PRESS

THE TRANSCENDENT MIRROR
A Bicentennial Anthology for Deerfield
Janet W. B. Rogers & Eric Widmer, Editors

Deerfield Academy Press
Old Main Street
Deerfield, Massachusetts 01342

ISBN 0-9632800-5-8
ISBN 0-9632800-6-6 pbk.

Library of Congress Cataloging-in-Publication Data

Transcendent mirror: a bicentennial anthology for Deerfield /
    edited by Janet W. B. Rogers and Eric Widmer
    Deerfield, Mass.: Deerfield Academy, 1999.
       p. : ill. ; cm
       1.Deerfield Academy, Deerfield, Mass. — History
    I. Rogers, Janet W. B. II. Widmer, Eric.
    LB1603-1695.D3622 1999
    373.222–dc20

Cover: *View from Albany Road*
1903-1917. Attributed to Ella (Childs) Enno
Memorial Hall Museum
Pocumtuck Valley Memorial Association
Deerfield, Massachusetts

CONTENTS

Preface

Janet W. B. Rogers

IN ASSEMBLING THIS ANTHOLOGY, WE FOUND OMISSION OUR MOST DIFFICULT TASK. Over the months of celebration, every program offered a wealth of information, reminiscence, professionalism, humor, inspiration and wisdom. In the end we based our choices on three criteria. The first was that the spoken material be readily convertible to clear written text; the second, that the subject matter be broad and various enough to speak to the interests of a wide Deerfield readership; the third, that the pieces fit naturally into our section groupings, so that the book itself would possess a logical structure. Inevitably, these criteria meant that some remarkable contributions missed inclusion, and for that necessity, we are sorry.

One notable and unavoidable omission in such a volume is the voice of the arts at Deerfield, wonderfully represented over the Bicentennial by exhibits, shows and performances that cannot be reproduced between these covers. The Homecoming and Grand Celebration programs, printed at the back of the book, record some of these extraordinary presentations from the visual and performing arts.

The panel discussions often took the shape of an hour or so of informal, wide-ranging conversation. To adapt them for this collection, we made transcriptions of audio tapes that had run during the programs, pruned them energetically and edited them into what we believe to be readable form. Overlappings and repetitions of memories, or of affection for the school and its stories, occurred naturally over the two-year stretch of celebration, and those we let stand.

This collection would not exist without the work of our partners in the enterprise. Mimi Morsman, Director of the Bicentennial, brought it all to vibrant life in the first place. In her office, Jessica Day and Sandy Yager transcribed with exquisite accuracy a massive quantity of unfamiliar audio tapes and other material. In particular, Sandy Yager proved her mettle on the video tape of President Bush's Commencement address. Sam Skillings and Ian Gracey made the tapes that keep our memories clear and green. Tina Cohen, Academy Archivist, shared treasures from her trove. Sandy Lively, who gets up awfully early in the morning, dedicated hours to scanning and transmitting nearly every printed text that speakers had given us. She then topped herself by doing a superb job of proofreading our manuscript, with superhuman precision. Sandy Ramsay, Executive Assistant to the Headmaster, kept all the wheels in motion with her inimitable gentle persistence and care. Robert and Andrea Moorhead, Directors of the Deerfield Academy Press, served as masterly guides, imaginative designers, and kind parents to the project.

To our contributors, listed along with their contributions and identified further at the back of the book, we owe our greatest thanks. As readers will see, our speakers devoted both expertise and sagacity to what they said to us. We are grateful beyond words, but we know that the words of this anthology speak for themselves.

Hilltop Farm
Deerfield, Massachusetts
May 1999

Introduction

Eric Widmer '57

From the day that the planning for the celebration of Deerfield Academy's two hundredth anniversary began, it was quite clear that we wanted to be looking forward and backward at the same time. We wanted to reflect in a thoughtful and serious way upon where, as a school, we had come from and where we were going, so that there would always be substance to our celebrations. The title of this book comes from the very last panel on the Grand Celebration Weekend of October 2-4, 1998: "The Transcendent Mirror: Deerfield at the Millennium."

When Meera Viswanathan suggested the title for that panel, she wanted to imply that there was indeed a way that Deerfield could see into the future by looking at the past. And we realized that that was how we were thinking of our Bicentennial, ever since the very first notice of the upcoming celebrations went out from me, with a letter saying that I hoped the Bicentennial would be remembered as a time when we remembered well.

The plan, as it took final shape, was to observe our great anniversary over a period of time that would allow all alumni a chance to come back and reacquaint themselves with their school. Six such homecomings were set in the calendar, each one specifically for a cadre of alumni, according to the decade in which they had graduated from Deerfield. The grand classes—our senior alumni up through the class of 1948—were all invited together to a special homecoming convocation in September, 1997.

At each of the six homecomings, one of our academic departments served as host and selected the topics of discussion for the Saturday seminar on that weekend. Returning alumni were invited to participate as panelists, and often chose to tie stories of decisions and accomplishments in their adult lives to early experiences at Deerfield. The discussions were invariably invigorating, and many of the contributions in this book were taken directly from them.

We often joked that since it took almost two years, from the granting of Deerfield's charter by Governor Samuel Adams and the Commonwealth of Massachusetts on March 1, 1797, to the actual opening of the Academy doors for the first time on January 1, 1799, we could certainly celebrate our Bicentennial for just as long. We began, appropriately enough, on "Charter Day," March 1, 1997. An extensive search had finally located the Deerfield charter in the archives of the State House in Boston. It was copied and presented to us by State Archivist John D. Warner, Jr., Deerfield Class of 1979, on Charter Day, when the whole school, all emeriti faculty who could be there, and invited townspeople marched behind the Eighth Massachusetts Fife and Drum Corps into the gymnasium.

A year and a half later, the Bicentennial observances ended with the Grand Celebration, easily the largest event of its kind ever undertaken by Deerfield. Eleven tents were pitched on campus, one running all the way from the Memorial Building to center field, and another covering the entire lawn behind the Academy Building. We had splendid entertainment and fireworks and food, and we had a series of excellent panel discussions that eloquently carried forward many of the themes that had already been part of our homecoming seminars.

This anthology is the result of our hope that the Deerfield Bicentennial could speak to everyone. Certainly we hope that in its pages will be found much of interest to the reader who cares about Deerfield specifically, or about education, or about the times in which we live. We have devised the chapters and their contents in such a way that the book moves between the general and the particular, but also with a progression from past/inward to future/outward. Those alumni and friends of Deerfield who attended some part of the celebrations will no doubt remember some of the presentations that have now found their way into this book. Others, who could not come back, will get a good sense of all the goings-on. In our *Transcendent Mirror*, in any case, we do hope you will find yourself reflected, along with the Deerfield of yesterday, today, and tomorrow.

The Manse
Deerfield, Massachusetts
May 1999

I. Deerfield at 200.

Wisdom is better than strength, beauty, and comely proportion; than health, long life, amusement and pleasure: It is better than monies, lands, mortgages and obligations; than rich trappings and splendid wardrobes. . . . And why shall men be commended according to their wisdom? For this simple reason, That wisdom renders men useful. . . . Nothing is important, or valuable, in the character of man, which does not render him beneficial to others, either by his example, or by his labours. . . .

The Reverend Joseph Lyman
The Advantages and Praises of Wisdom
A sermon delivered at the opening of Deerfield Academy
New Year's Day 1799

View from Albany Road

1903-1917 Photograph attributed to Ella (Childs) Fenno
Memorial Hall Museum
Pocumtuck Valley Memorial Association
Deerfield, Massachusetts

Alice and Warren Ilchman gave the Bicentennial Address at the
Grand Celebration Convocation on October 2, 1998,
having spent a month in residence on campus as Deerfield's Bicentennial Fellows.
They delivered the sections of their speech in turns.

DEERFIELD AT 200: ACHIEVEMENTS AND OPPORTUNITIES

Alice S. Ilchman P'85 and Warren F. Ilchman P '85

LOYAL SONS AND DAUGHTERS OF DEERFIELD, proud alumni and parents, talented teachers, Headmaster Widmer, trustees, new friends and colleagues of this most gracious Academy: In a weekend packed with events that have been several years in the planning, and in celebration of events two centuries in the making, and with a new millennium in prospect, we are pleased to offer the Bicentennial Address.

It is a daunting assignment. We have, however, received a small reassurance. In 1947, the sesquicentennial celebration featured two formal addresses—one by the Headmaster of Phillips Academy and the second by a Harvard professor. Both looked to the past and to the future of the independent school—or so we think. In the otherwise impeccable Deerfield archives, a copy of neither speech could be found. And if that is the future for Bicentennial speeches, the task already seems a little less daunting.

So even if the world little notes, and can never again find, what we say here, we hope that these ideas, woven with the dozens of other ideas in the current discourse within the school, may signal a renewal of the purposes and methods of Deerfield Academy.

We thought we knew Deerfield Academy pretty well. We are Deerfield parents; each of us had taught at or headed educational institutions that assiduously courted Deerfield graduates; I once served as trustee of a boarding school that is a rival to Deerfield; and Warren Ilchman taught the Headmaster, one Eric Widmer, at Williams College in the late 1950s.

These connections, however, pale before the opportunities given to Bicentennial Fellows really to know Deerfield. In three weeks, we have become well acquainted. We attended some 41 classes—introductory and advanced, required and elective, across the entire curriculum, from the arts to the sciences. We tracked the daily schedule of four different students, including their sit-down meals, college advising, and band practice. We watched athletic scrimmages and attended meetings for new faculty. We interviewed all the living headmasters. We talked and talked—and listened and listened—to members of the faculty and retirees, dorm corridor counselors, international students, admissions directors and deans, and with visiting school heads from faraway countries.

I showed up for my sport, rec tennis, and, alas, we missed some appointments and collected a few "APs" ("accountability points"). We read issues of *The Scroll* from 1985 to the present, consulted the archives, and, in good Deerfield style, we kept a journal. If all this was necessary to know the true Deerfield, it was nevertheless not yet sufficient. So in search of the heart of the enterprise, we watched Dottie and Norm give out athletic equipment, picked apples at Clarkdale on Heritage Day, and joined the opening convocation to sing "The Deerfield Evensong" under the timeless direction of Mr. Peter Hindle. With this we rest our case as Bicentennial participant-observers.

What do we wish to note about Deerfield at age 200? We want to make four points. The first is expected of observers who themselves come from education—an answer to the question of how well is Deerfield fulfilling its mission as a college preparatory school, and as the formal educator in some subjects of last experience for its graduates? The latter is especially pertinent, for many subjects are not pursued at the college level and what Deerfield does in introducing and advancing them must stand for life's formal instruction in those fields.

For alumni and parents, and others committed to Deerfield Academy, let us unequivocally state that in our view there could be no better instruction than that offered here. There is equivalent education elsewhere, perhaps, but nothing better than what we found in our class visits. From the design of the curriculum and the organization of learning to immediate pedagogy in the classroom, from what is expected from students and what is received, instruction at Deerfield is the very best—authoritative in content, but welcoming of new research, formidable but accessible, serious but seductive.

We believe Deerfield graduates will enter college better prepared than their contemporaries and better equipped to build on what they know. Nor should we fear that subjects never formally studied after Deerfield will leave a graduate inadequately prepared to participate in the duties of the citizen, or remain self-educating. Quite the contrary. It seems to us that the subjects such as math, sciences, and the arts pursued here are university-worthy and, even if they are the culminating course in the student's experience in these subjects, they contain every prospect for continuing self-instruction.

What appears to the outsider as exceptionally high quality is obviously the product of hundreds of compromises, treaties, adjustments on the part of faculty, and the apparently infinite willingness, on the part of students, to forego sleep. The calendar is unforgiving, as are the pressures for advanced placement, athletics, college visits, co-curricular activities and just plain living. How these are all blended together into a positive whole—if not necessarily every day for the individual faculty member or student—is the Deerfield way of education.

The Deerfield way is worth pausing over. It is more than a prepared student and a prepared faculty member in an environment that encourages learning and teaching. It includes a constructive emphasis on industriousness and the respect for student autonomy in some areas, such as athletics, but less in others, such as the academic choice of what is intellectually important. It also contains one value that appears to be the prime motivator of faculty here: Deerfield faculty members consider the failure of a student to be a failure of a faculty member as well.

This balance between autonomy and industriousness and the widespread assumption of common responsibility in the success of the student seem to us to be key features of the Deerfield way and quite emulatable. To be emulated, however, requires the approach to be describable. As observers, we find the Deerfield way of instruction tacit and intuited, but seldom discussed. We find Deerfield faculty to be unself-conscious about what they do and how they do it. The Deerfield way is not found in a faculty handbook; nor is it the subject of faculty orientation. With the very large degree of autonomy of faculty in what they teach, it is hard to know where faculty acquire such unanimity in how they approach their pedagogy. But they do.

If it were discussed and if it were part of, say, faculty orientation, the Deerfield way could become an important occasion to share values. It might then be discussed how to overcome the otherwise unforgiving quality of the calendar, and how to balance the college-bound imperatives with what rounds out a high school experience. It might also become the occasion to discuss whether the degree of respect for the autonomy of the student should vary by subject matter, or whether industriousness as a virtue is always virtuous.

It may well be asked what Deerfield has to say to the national debate on high school in the United States. First, to call it a national debate on high school is to mislabel it. Our once nationwide concern with the common school has been replaced by dozens of advocates of reform speaking past each other. It is worth noting, however, that what you have achieved in this valley is what would delight liberals and conservatives alike—the role of content in education, the importance of values, the constructive autonomy of teachers, and a strong Head. Ted Sizer's Horace Smith need make few compromises at Deerfield. Only those critics who claim that good education must arise out of the student's urgent questions, not from a content-driven curriculum, would say that Deerfield neglected that important source.

Our second point would be that, in what seems to be a timeless formula for good education, the Academy has, nonetheless, sought to make this very good school even better. (Mr. Lambert, I think I need that "very.") Using the benchmark of 1985, when we last saw the school closely through our son, we would like to focus on four developments. Each of these additions, we believe, has made Deerfield a stronger place, more useful in educating young people to this time.

Although these agendas—coeducation, a diverse community, the growth of the arts, and community service—are not finished, indeed one never "finishes" an agenda in human relations or social progress, we give high marks to the goals but sometimes lower marks to the progress towards some of them.

For coeducation we give three cheers. To all of us who knew and loved the Deerfield Boy, it is gratifying, but not really surprising, to find the Deerfield Girl is clearly his peer. While rising numbers of strong applications and increasing parity in ratios between boys and girls tell one very positive story, they do not, in themselves, tell us whether Deerfield "feels" to students like an effectively functioning coeducational school. In our minds and on the basis of our visit here, it does. While some language may need to be adjusted, the symbols of hospitality for coeducation are abundant and clear. Let us just say that we found every indication that careful planning, learning from the mistakes of others, humility in the task, imaginative thinking and generous action have given Deerfield a productive and welcoming coeducational environment.

An equally welcome change is the role of the arts in the curriculum and school life. The evidence is all around us this weekend of that increasing presence. As you know well, Deerfield is a full plate. It is not easy to add anything more. Compared to the mid 80s, when we listened to our viola player in a struggling string quartet, the arts have developed with considerable confidence. New faculty have been appointed; a new arts building has been constructed; an ambitious theatrical season is a community expectation; and a whole new subject, Dance, has taken its place in the curriculum.

I offer two vignettes, one we observed, the other we were told about. Imagine fifty-six players in the concert band, that is some five soccer teams (or half the size of the New York Philharmonic), playing recognizable Bach. Imagine a dance piece, performed by fourteen male students, choreographed by one of their classmates. Why is it important to push the arts for students, when so much else of value already fills their days? The arts, as efficiently as any subject, teach students the connection between discipline and creativity. The arts open the mind to new ways of thinking, and help us cross the fault lines of social difference by giving a universal human experience.

Getting into college is important, but not at the expense of getting a life. Coaches and teachers, please make room. Cooperation, as well as competition, is intrinsic to growth and maturity. We hope also that more coaches and faculty alike can make room for Community Service. Living here with you, we have become sensitive to the tyranny of the clock, the limitations of the school day. Students' time is Deerfield's scarcest resource, with faculty time a close second. You offer so many competing good options for the limited time and attention of students. The schedule is so full that even efforts toward high achievement, such as advanced placement courses, can have negative impact on other goals.

It is impressive, then, that you have made space for a co-curricular activity, Community Service. Since 1986, the Academy has put increasing resources of time and talent into these programs. For the last three years the entire academy has been mobilized for the service projects that make up Heritage Day. Some 40-50 students and faculty supervisors, significantly here called Deerfield coaches, regularly perform Community Service as a co-curricular activity. At least two speakers on tomorrow's panel can give testimony to the value of such experience.

Suffice it to say that data across many institutions show that Community Service, well planned and adequately supervised, allows students to test theory against practice, gives them a context for analyzing complex problems, and, perhaps most important, can demonstrate the power of the individual to make social change. Community Service is not just good works. It can be superb education. Yet it remains a peripheral experience for most students and faculty at Deerfield. Almost no member of the faculty has made service learning essential to her or his course. It would be our hope that the Bicentennial Fellows of 2008 find a Dottie and a Norm issuing needed equipment to community service volunteers and a host of buses headed toward food kitchens and Habitats in Greenfield and Holyoke.

In the fourth area of change, building a diverse campus, we give only two cheers. It could be argued that Deerfield has long been diverse—economically and geographically. But for students of color, many schools like Deerfield started late. Indeed, Deerfield's first black graduate was taught by Warren Ilchman at Williams, as recently as the 1960s. At the same time we want to note that this year's convocation looked far different in composition from the 1985 commencement when our son graduated. With some 20 per cent of the student body students of color, Deerfield has made commendable progress in only a few years. We know that success is more than numbers. The Deerfield emphasis on personal respect and group civility are strong allies in this goal.

A tougher problem, and one of which the deans and faculty colleagues are well aware, is the answer to the question asked by students of color, "Why, on the faculty and staff, are there not more faces that look like mine?" There are reasonable answers. But it is not yet good enough for Deerfield. Deerfield needs more authority figures who are persons of color if we are about the business of educating young people who will make a positive difference in others' lives—one definition of leadership. This agenda must be addressed, again and again. Recognizing that Deerfield can make few new appointments each year, the recruitment of this more diverse faculty, like all faculty, requires leadership from the top, patience, imagination, and optimism. Perhaps it will also require a Deerfield solution, of "growing your own." But it must happen.

What might be future directions for Deerfield? Let us suggest two possibilities that this community might consider for the new century. Both are only "names," but in their implementation there are many options to achieve a different, though not necessarily better, Deerfield.

The first option is for the Academy to think of itself as a national school. In our debate over the common school and the achievement of a national standard, we have neglected the possibility that there already exist within this country "national schools," one of which is Deerfield. These schools offer a curriculum that is seen by selective colleges as valuable; they draw their student bodies nationally; their students go off to study nationally; and the whole nation, if not the world, is where their graduates undertake their later work.

To be more self-conscious in this role would be a possible goal for Deerfield in the next century. What might this include? First and foremost, it would require making known, alone or with other national schools in this country, that Deerfield aspires to play a national standard-setting role. It would recruit systematically from the whole country, going beyond those who would ordinarily apply, to an energetic effort to insure, through whatever means, a national composition.

Rather than be whipsawed by what others require—from advanced placement programs to other standard setters—Deerfield would become a school, or among schools, that expect to set the standard—the best that American schools should seek. The scores of its graduates would not need to be the highest; the curricular objectives, however, would be the standard to be obtained by others. It would mean taking on some national priorities—e.g., encouraging more to enter science and technology or public service—and including those objectives among the objectives of the Academy. It would mean making common cause with schools that play this role elsewhere in the world.

Why would this role be desirable? In the first place, it gives Deerfield a bully pulpit to help set standards for what Deerfield has found of value. Second, it would give greater salience to Deerfield admissions. It could make graduation from a national school to be as prestigious as graduation from an Ivy League college.

An alternative role to consider at this juncture in your history is to be among the first of the global schools. By this, we mean something different from the host of international schools that exist in capital cities around the world. For good or often for ill, we live globally. Financial capital, taste, entertainment, fashion, disease, and tranquillity, all happen or are defined by forces outside of one country. Borders delay but do not contain. When one looks at the student body of Deerfield, not simply the students who come from abroad, but the many US-based students whose parents have emigrated to this country, there are clear signs that this is what Deerfield is already becoming—a global school.

While others intend to play this role—the International Baccalaureate schools and more particularly the United World Colleges—they have not been rooted in a place with a reputation as strong as Deerfield's, nor do they focus on high school alone. As many international parents are selecting American colleges as the destination for their children, a global school that is simultaneously an American high school would be doubly attractive.

We fancy there is some 21st century Frank Boyden taking the headship somewhere of an independent school which has lived beyond its founding definition, with that goal in mind, just as a 20th century Frank Boyden took on a dying New England academy and made it the best of what it now is. Perhaps the same process is afoot, and why not here? Recruitment of the student body would become more deliberately global, and heavily supported. Subject matter would need to become more cosmopolitan to reflect the more varied destinations of graduates. Languages would become more prominent. Co-curricular opportunities might expand to accommodate the more diverse interests—new sports would be played, new art forms presented. And as before, Deerfield might need to make common cause with those other schools that are being called upon to play a global role.

Why should this even be entertained? First, the possibility to become such a place is already present at Deerfield. Second, the education of American students in the environment of the global school would be enhanced. Third, it provides the leadership role in secondary education that Deerfield has the human resources to undertake.

Whatever is chosen as a future path, you must always remember that where you are today, what you are in fact celebrating this weekend, was the vision of a person who had a mission, a sense of timing, and an understanding of what society needed. Rather than just sniffing at these possibilities, go for them.

The educational initiatives committee for the Bicentennial produced some tantalizing options for new ways to educate. We have proposed a notion or two, but anyone entertaining change for Deerfield, without a clear sense of what is essential, what is intrinsic to Deerfield, does so with peril.

We have tried to distill what might make up the essence of the Deerfield tradition (and we do this at our peril). But what is it then, that without which, it would not be Deerfield? Everyone has a view, from the newest members of the community, to those who have lived with it the longest. Right at the top, we believe, is sustaining the sense of place. What is Deerfield without the main street, clapboard houses, mountains, river, and sunset on 100 ancient windows? Peter Fallon has already given us this vision and a cornucopia of metaphors.

Cognizant of living in a global society, we must nonetheless protect the gifts of a deeply-American, deeply-New England academy. Whatever is considered in the future, you must have central to your endeavor the preservation, the renewal, and the incorporation of this place in your activities. It is an endowment beyond value. A recently published book about Deerfield homelots illustrates starkly the importance of tearing down and building up. Page after page shows homesteads acquired by the Academy and protected with new uses, or acquired by the Academy and torn down for other uses. Protecting the sense of place, as you—the Academy, Historic Deerfield and townsfolk—know intimately, is not the simple formula of preserving a perfect moment. Protection is dynamic; it is tearing down and building up. Your choices will matter a great deal.

Second, we believe that the size of the school, the numbers of individuals who make up this face-to-face community, is not a trivial matter. It is an issue we find that headmasters for half a century have felt keenly about. Whether the metaphor is the family, or a caring community, it makes a difference if the family can all sit down to dinner together; indeed, the *Christian Science Monitor* once found that the high school students most likely to make honor roll came from families that sat down together at dinner.

The numbers are not arbitrary—how many students fit around a seminar table? fill an auditorium? It is a deeply held value here that if you can get the school together physically, you can hold it together. With our Yankee commitment to efficiency, growth in numbers is seductive. And there is a missionary drive, no doubt, to give every superb candidate a chance at this education. Small increases adding up all of a sudden to a big increase may be as pernicious as bold plans for growth. You have told us, and we know this from our own knowledge, of the very different character of boarding schools that are significantly larger than Deerfield. Can you franchise Deerfield? Should not a model be reproduced? Possibly, and the greatest compliment to a school is its imitators. But consider a bigger school at your peril.

The third of these irreducible minimums seems to us to be the commitment to and the cherishing by the adults of the total education of young people. Even in the labor-intensive world of the independent boarding school, the willingness of adults to invest longer hours and more care in the development of young citizens and moral human beings is marked. From this commitment and sense of common purpose flow other essential attributes—civility, loyalty, and pride. How to keep this model civil society alive and fresh may be your most subtle task.

To sum up what we are about: the Bicentennial, long in the planning and 200 years in the making, has as its purpose reflection, celebration, and just plain fun. We hope we have added to the reflection. In addition, we hope that our contribution conforms to what Robert McGlynn found expressive of Deerfield's 1947 Sesquicentennial pageant, and I quote: "An event of characteristic simple dignity, effortless ordering, and friendly spirit—the very ingredients of the community they celebrated."

This panel discussion took place on October 3, 1998,
during the Grand Celebration weekend
as part of "The School's Program for Our Alumni."

REFRACTING THE PAST: RECONSIDERATIONS OF OUR HISTORY

Thomas G. Clark '67P, Charles E. Danielski '53, Donald R. Friary P'92, '93,
Karinne T. Heise, Thomas A. Heise, Brian A. Rosborough '58P

Brian A. Rosborough '58P, Moderator. We're going to be looking at history through different lenses, refracting history. In preparation for today, I looked up what Mr. Emerson had to say about history. In what was then called the "Academic Declaration of Independence," he said that we have "squandered our resources in this foolish lust for the past, while under our boots lies abundant material for the appreciation of the arts, life and character. The literature of the poor, the feelings of a child, the philosophy of the street, the meaning of household life, these are the topics of time," he said. And he went on to say, "How else will we know about the pan of milk, the ballad in the street, the glance of the eye, or the gait and form of the body?" Now I don't think Mr. Emerson got out much, but he was saying that we should look at history from a local perspective. I might ask Tom Heise to get us mixed up in this. What about your lust for the past? Why do we study history? Why is it so important?

Thomas A. Heise. I think that historians have generally valued history because they believe that it provides wisdom, individually by extending our own range of experience and collectively by allowing us to know as a society where we've been and what we've come from. There are also those of us who find it fun, and we're a strange lot that can't be trusted!

Donald R. Friary P'92, '93. I think there's another dimension that really cuts through the ages. The historian teaches and writes history to seek wisdom and to pass it on. But I think much of history is consumer driven, which is a rather modern term. I would say that people have studied history, have passed it on, have recorded it, in order to give themselves definition as individuals, where there is individual heroic history or a family history.

And as a community, as a culture, people define themselves by their histories. Sometimes these turn into legends of origins, but very often they are quite specific, "This is who we are because this is where we came from"; and that becomes awfully important to individuals and communities. Of course it refers to verbal history, but also to the history that's all around us in a place like Deerfield—the landscape, man's impact on the landscape.

Rosborough. Does the past define the present or is it the other way around?

Karinne T. Heise. The lens I'd refract that through is the lens of literature. I think of Toni Morrison's *Beloved*, in which the relationship of people to their history is very different from our relationship under this tent when we're looking at our "Days of Glory." In that novel, the protagonist's relationship to her past is a horrible one. Her memories of slavery, her memories of infanticide, have created a physical ghost in her life, which is real. And it haunts her so much that her sense of self is almost completely consumed.

When Morrison leaves us at the end of the novel with this litany of "It is not a story to pass on. It is not a story to pass on. This is not a story to pass on," it is ironic because she actually does pass on the story by writing the novel. Depending on what your history is, your relationship to it is very different. In this case, this woman's past so defined her that she has almost nothing left. She doesn't have the power to define her past, which is often what we do. We've labeled our history for this Bicentennial "Days of Glory," because we have the power to do so.

Friary. But she does define it: she does so in a negative way. And that's one of the important things about studying history. We should be looking at the negative—where we've failed—as well as where we've succeeded, and find out why, what there is in the human condition that creates those failures.

T. Heise. I think that history, if it's going to remain a vital discipline, has to be revised constantly. A fairly good example of this, I think, is the impact of the 1960s on the way that US history has been written and included in textbooks. Prior to the 60s most standard US history textbooks told a fairly familiar story about presidents and great political conflicts. After the 1960s . . . for example, the textbook that I use now devotes at least half of its pages to the stories of people who, prior to the 60s, were not included.

Rosborough. Is history really an accurate predictor of the future?

T. Heise. Certainly not! If it were, I think we wouldn't be as surprised as we are. I think all history can do is suggest a range of possibilities.

Thomas G. Clark '67P. At Deerfield I know there's an American Studies Program that combines literature and American history, and then there's the River, Valley, Rock course. Is that the direction Deerfield is going in, to be more interdisciplinary in history?

T. Heise. There's a strong institutional interest in doing that. It also depends on finding faculty who have that interest. But we have found that those courses work very, very well. I would add that history is a discipline that, if it's rightly understood, is utterly interdisciplinary to start with. It's about us and all that we do.

Rosborough. Aha, who is "us"? The 300 generations of Native Americans who've been in this valley; do they invade your stories here, Karinne?

K. Heise. They do on occasion. Probably we don't teach enough Native American literature yet. The tradition is so oral that it's difficult to find as many written works to choose from as one might like. It's interesting when you think about that culture's relationship to history versus our culture's relationship to history. I would be curious to know if history was even a part of the Native American vocabulary, since it seems to be such a fluid part of their existence. The past and the present were intertwined in a very organic way.

Charles E. Danielski '53. But interestingly in this valley, we have the legend of Beaver Ridge. . . . For a long time the Indians had a legend that if you stepped back a mile or so to the West and looked back at the ridge that is Mount Sugarloaf about seven or eight miles south of us and the next ridge called North Sugarloaf, and then the long protrusion of Pocumtuck Ridge, you would have the impression of looking at a beaver that was swimming in a lake, a beaver that had been speared by an Indian and drifted out into the lake. And the view really is very much like a beaver from a distance, the profile. That was discounted or just thought to be an interesting legend for a long time.

Then Edward Hitchcock, the geologist who was also a headmaster at Deerfield in the early 1800s, discovered evidence of a huge glacial lake that occupied this area for probably 4,000 years. During that period of time the ridge would have been a series of islands in a really great-sized lake. But it was still thought that American indigenous people hadn't been here for more than 3,000 years. About 20 years ago, they were building an industrial park in South Deerfield, and getting government funds to support it. By government decree they had to bring in archaeologists to do test sites so that they weren't going to blacktop over something that was of archaeological interest. At that point they found the remains of an encampment that radioactively dated to over 10,500 years ago. That tripled the age of anything that had been found east of the Mississippi. Then people began realizing perhaps the great glacial lake was just drying up when these people arrived, and very possibly the land did look like an immense beaver. I think what's really exciting to think about is, if that is so, it's an oral tradition that's been passed on for 10,000 years. [For Brian Rosborough's opinion on this subject, see page 40.]

Clark. The interesting thing for me about that is, here I live on the hillside of Old Deerfield and everybody thinks of Old Deerfield as being down here in the village. But what happened was probably that the indigenous people who came through the area, after the glacier receded and the lake was here, had to live on the banks of the lake; they didn't live down here; this was flooded. So actually people lived where I live before they came down here. In fact, when Lake Hitchcock was here, there was still silt on top of where we are now.

This was a story passed on to me by my father and another woman who lived in the area, who's probably in her nineties now. She told about her grandparents in the late 1800s, who every summer would have visitors, a Canadian Indian couple that would migrate down to the valley, camp on the hillside, make baskets and bring them to Old Deerfield and sell them. They'd been doing this, I guess, for generations, migrating down from Canada, whether or not they had any relationship to the people who had been captured and had gone back to Canada. But they were still going to the same place on the hill to get the basket material and camping in the same area. So there was a continuum, and I guess we are re-writing history because in Old Deerfield there's been more thought about the Native Americans and what their interaction was with the English people when they came here. The Indians didn't die out completely and disappear. They were just like immigrants that came in later, the Germans and the Poles; they gradually got mixed into society.

K. Heise. It's also self-selection, if you choose to identify yourself as a Native American. But what I found interesting about the story of the beaver is the way the story is connected to a part of the landscape and that strong sense of place that not only emanates from or infuses the world of the Native American, but also, as the Ilchmans were saying last night, infuses Deerfield today. That is one of the things that we really should hold onto: our sense of place.

Rosborough. In my work we know that there are maybe 6,000 spoken languages of which 3,000 will survive the century. 728 will be spoken in Papua New Guinea. Another 625 will be spoken in Indonesia. So the diversity of language and thought and oral tradition is narrowing down to a very few places around the world. What does that say about your work? In European History and US History, are we too ethnocentric about the way we communicate history to the young today?

T. Heise. I think we are less ethnocentric all the time. There have been considerable and successful efforts in the last 30 years or so to include a much greater range of people and cultures in our study of the past. I also think that a study of local history can be done the same way. A great number of different peoples have lived in this valley and interacted, and so this is yet another way that a study of place can suggest a broader, more inclusive vision of what we once were than we've traditionally done.

Friary. History is by its very nature ethnocentric because we are studying ourselves. But the interesting thing about history is that we are studying ourselves in another time—we're studying our ancestors. And we discover that they are in fact other people. In many ways they are like us, just as the people in Papua New Guinea are like us in many ways, but the more we learn about them the more we find those differences.

Rosborough. Charlie, how did the River, Valley, Rock course go, from your perspective as someone who bridges both the physical sciences and the biological sciences?

Danielski. Very successfully: the blending of the disciplines gives the students a much wider perspective, and the opening and broadening of perspective is part of the educational process. The course also provides the opportunity to get out—they do so on a weekly basis. They're in the field for over two hours a week, traversing the valley, viewing it from different angles and trying to get a feel for more than just The Street.

Rosborough. For about 100 years, weather and warfare had a lot to do with the survival and livelihoods of people who lived here. Does that change with time?

Clark. The paleolithic peoples settled here because they were hunter-gatherers, but then they gradually became farmers. And they came here because of the good soil. It was a great place to grow things and continues to be. There are still three farm families that border Deerfield Academy and have many relationships with it: the Williams on the South, and the Savages on the West, and the Yazwinskis on the North. We're fortunate that this land is kept open by the farmers. Even before River, Valley, Rock, there was a sense of more reaching out from Deerfield Academy and learning about the surroundings. Heritage Day is part of it, getting the students aware of where they are. It's not just Main Street in Old Deerfield, it's the town of Deerfield, it's Franklin County, it's Western Massachusetts.

Danielski. This place is so rich in geology that they bring students here from Harvard and Princeton and Yale. Princeton makes a six-hour bus ride to come to Deerfield to look at the geology. That was part of the feeling that Frank Boyden had and projected so unbelievably powerfully to the students —to appreciate the place, the sense of place, to be worthy of something.

Friary. And it's not just a sense of place here. By acquiring this sense of place, by learning what we do from the landscape and the villagescape and the geology, we are learning to read those things elsewhere.

K. Heise. One of the things that we often do in the English Department is to try to help students connect themselves to this place in particular, and places in general, through their writing. Teachers will take their students to the graveyard, or the Rock or the river. I like to take them to the Yazwinski farm, where we just missed the birthing of a calf this fall. They get a fuller sense of the sensory details of this place, which they incorporate in their writing, but also, I hope, absorb in deeper ways as well.

Rosborough. What I've been hearing is that there's something about the spirit here that is bigger than the place, bigger than us, bigger than the generations of people that were here. It's a moral geography, if you will, a blend of history and myth that represents values that we all either aspire to or feel we've lost. And that's why places like Deerfield are so important to the soul and such fertile grounds for educating people and for growing "apples" who go off to do other things. I wanted to talk a little about the capacities here in the valley, to see if we can learn here anything at all about, let's say, the management of food, soil and water. Could you teach us a little bit about food, soil, and water if you were on the faculty, Tom?

K. Heise. What are these bags of apples for, Tom?

Clark. I thought about this last night after I heard Alice and Warren Ilchman talk about how they propose that we become a national school and a global school, but I think we shouldn't lose track of being a local school too. What the apples represent: I've got three varieties here that we grow. The first one to your left was discovered in the 30s by a man who worked for the Civilian Conservation Corps. In taking down old apple trees that were going to cause problems to orchards that were nearby, he found these apples and named them after himself. They're called the Davey and are only grown in Massachusetts, to my knowledge. The middle variety is called Empire, a cross between Red Delicious and Macintosh, developed in New York State and grown throughout the United States, but to my knowledge, very little elsewhere in the world. And the variety closest to me is called Gala. It's for this festivity that we're in now. This was developed in New Zealand 20-25 years ago and became so popular that it was exported to Europe and is now grown everywhere in the world. And this is how we're teaching, how we're relating the school and history together. They form a good mix, in my mind. They're different, and yet they're equals, and this is how the school ought to go. You can't lose your sense of place: teaching local history, having local people involved in the school.

Rosborough. Food, and the growing of apples, because it's so darned hard to get 'em to be pretty, can teach us a little bit about chemical dependency, chemicals and land, chemicals and people, herbicides and pesticides.

Clark. We have done a lot of work with the University of Massachusetts on something called Integrated Pest Management. It isn't organic agriculture, but it's minimal chemical usage on crops. It started on apples in Massachusetts and then developed for strawberries, corn and everything else. You're spraying a minimum amount of a toxic pesticide that would have any impact on the environment. We do a lot of trapping; we do a lot of weather monitoring. So we're using a minimum amount of toxic material but growing a very good crop that people will buy. Because if you tried to grow an organic apple in Massachusetts, especially in a year like this, you wouldn't have a crop. It rained every day for the first two weeks in May, during pollination time, and all the blossoms either fell off, or they got scab on the apples. People abandoned organic orchards, but we've got a crop.

Rosborough. We've got people in the audience who are associated with the Deerfield Land Trust. We talked a little bit yesterday about the addition of about 90 million new passengers a year on the planet. They all seem to want to live in this valley now.

Friary. This is something we do learn from the history of Deerfield. Deerfield was a planned community at the very beginning. It was not something that just happened. There were surveyors who laid out the town. The village is on the plateau. The farmland is surrounding it. For the economic base in agriculture, but also for defense and to create a community, this was all very carefully planned. And we should keep on planning.

Mark Zenick (Executive Director, Deerfield Land Trust, from the audience). We work with farmers because farmers are the best stewards and land conservationists around. The 1990 census was the first time in this country that farmers weren't listed as a vocation, as an employment category, because the category fell beneath 2%. In this country, that is an interesting trend, because farmers are responsible, especially here in Deerfield, for maintaining much of this remarkable landscape. I think everyone who comes back to visit or lives here or walks here through the seasons is reminded that if we lose that connection with the landscape, with the buildings, with the history, then in a human way we've lost something essential, and culturally, spiritually we'll be lessened. So the idea of respecting history and protecting what we have is a significant endeavor.

Danielski (responding to a question about the Deerfield River). One of the problems the Academy has right now is trying to understand the Deerfield River enough to be able to preserve the Lower Level. The river is beginning to look like it may start to reclaim some of our playing fields. The old way, which was done in the 30s when Frank Boyden was here, was to dump a lot of rocks on the edge of the river and not allow it to move. People have begun to realize that if you do that, all you do is pass your problems on to the next person down the line, and the power of the river doesn't diminish by eating your land away; it focuses on the next person down river. So that's no longer a viable alternative. There are groups that Deerfield is working with to try to understand how can we maintain a river bank without, again, going beyond our own ecological address and affecting somebody else.

Rosborough. I took a look at Bruce Barton's wonderful comments of years ago, where he described the school to the family and community who supported the school. He talked about many of the things that we've been talking about all weekend long and concluded that geographers tell us that where men live has a tremendous influence on what they are. Of the New Englanders, he attributed strength of character to the granite in the hills. They were makers of institutions he thought. He concluded by saying that "Deerfield really is the cradle of this kind of spirit," the spirit of place that we've been talking about. He said, "You can't purchase it. You can't even create it. It's something unseen in the ancient halls of this place and on the hillsides that surround us." He felt that character covers the campus like a mantle, and the difference between right and wrong thrusts itself across the horizon as inescapably as Mount Tom.

II. THE PLACE AND ITS PAST.

The logical place to start from is home. As highlighted in the panel discussion, "Refracting the Past," one of Deerfield's great strengths is its natural and historical environment. Grounded in this valley, centered in its teaching here, the school at the same time extends its reach beyond the village.

Deerfield Academy Reunion—1879

Unidentified photographer
Memorial Hall Museum
Pocumtuck Valley Memorial Association
Deerfield, Massachusetts

Tom Heise gave this talk to new students on September 13, 1998,
welcoming them to the Academy in the final year of Bicentennial observances.
Here he encapsulates the history of the region and the school.
The three contributions that follow expand on Tom's topics.

A DEERFIELD WELCOME

Thomas A. Heise

ON THIS OCCASION WE WELCOME YOU TO A NEW COMMUNITY AND A NEW PLACE. ONE of the ways in which we extend our welcome is to tell you a little about the history of Deerfield and of people who were here before you. You probably have all noticed that one way you become friends with someone else is to learn about that person's past; as we share personal histories, we forge friendships. We hope that tonight we can begin to invite you into a friendship with this place that will last well beyond the time that you spend here.

I would like to enlist your imaginations as I tell you just a little about Deerfield—about the valley in which we are so lucky to live, the village in which we reside, and the Academy in which we all play a part. A sense of history, after all, requires not only evidence but also the capacity to imagine yourself in another time and setting among people who may have been very different than you are. So imagine what you might have seen and experienced here, had you arrived in Deerfield just a little bit earlier.

Had you stumbled into Deerfield 190 million years ago, you would have been greeted by spectacular mountain views and an alluring tropical climate. But you would have been competing for space with a Deerfield "student body" that was large, carnivorous, and hungry. Your Deerfield "classmates" would have been dinosaurs, easy prey for you in the classroom but awfully scary in the afternoon out on the fields. If you had the terrible misfortune to be in this spot 20,000 years ago, you would now be frozen solid, locked in the ice sheet that descended over much of North America during our last ice age.

Had you arrived here 13,000 years ago and sat where you are sitting now, you would now be holding your breath—desperately—for you would have been sitting underwater, on the bottom of Lake Hitchcock, a glacial lake that filled the Connecticut Valley from Rocky Hill, Connecticut to St. Johnsbury, Vermont for perhaps a thousand or more years.

Had you come to this place four hundred years ago, you would have encountered a very different and long-established culture. In 1600, this was the home of the Pocumtuck Indians, a confederacy perhaps 1,500 strong who farmed this land and fought to protect it, who hunted and hiked these hills, who watched the sun come up over the ridge to the east and set over the mountains to the west, just as you will. The Pocumtucks and their predecessors cultivated this valley for over 1,000 years; Native Americans inhabited this valley for nearly 10,000 years, a history that makes the three-hundred-year-old village of Deerfield seem almost new.

If you had arrived three hundred years ago for the purpose of attending a residential liberal arts high school that prepared students for college, you would have been laughed out of town. Such an institution would have seemed to Deerfield residents an almost inconceivable luxury. At the close of the seventeenth century, worries about an impending attack on Deerfield by Indians began to mount. Early in the morning of February 29, 1704, the attack came. French and Indian forces fell on Deerfield, killing more than fifty people and carrying over 100 townspeople into captivity. This was Deerfield's most violent day in a blood-soaked span of nearly forty years that saw this tiny frontier village suffer repeated attacks, in attempts by Indians and the French to displace the English settlers who lived here.

Had you come to Deerfield two hundred years ago, you would have been arriving at the very beginning of this institution. The Academy's founding might be viewed as a hopeful, even triumphant, conclusion to a century in Deerfield that clearly had begun dismally. Deerfield Academy was founded in 1797, one of a number of academies existing throughout New England that were all the region had to offer in the way of high school education; the fully articulated public education system that we know today would not come about until nearly one hundred years after the founding of this Academy. None of the buildings that you see on campus today was part of that school. Admission was open to boys and girls, ranging in age from ten to twenty-one, with just one catch: the unexacting requirement that students had to be "capable of reading and writing." Within a couple of years, student enrollment edged up towards one hundred. Tuition was usually less than ten dollars a year, with additional charges for firewood. A Deerfield education, according to Bob and Andrea Moorhead's recently published *Deerfield 1797-1997: A Pictorial History of the Academy*, was practical, designed for students "who would spend only a few terms in school before going to work on the farm or in business."

Had you arrived one hundred years ago, you would have learned that Deerfield Academy was in danger of fading away forever—its destiny, apparently, to be an unremarkable footnote in the history of a town that was itself languishing after a half-century decline (and that you should have gone to one of the other schools to which you were accepted!). At the turn of the century, only fourteen students attended the school, at least four of whom, writes John McPhee, "were regarded with fear." The Academy was presided over by trustees who were locally unpopular and whose management of the school's finances was more than a little suspect. No centennial celebration took place at all in 1898 for fear that it would invite unwelcome public scrutiny of the Board of Trustees.

In 1902, the fortunes of Deerfield Academy changed forever on the day, continues McPhee, that Frank L. Boyden "walked downhill into the town for the first time nodding, as he moved along, to women in full-length skirts, girls in petticoats, and little boys wearing long-sleeved shirts and bowler hats," turned onto Deerfield's dusty, wheel-rutted main street, saw its two-hundred-year-old farm houses and its dispirited little school, and took on the job as Headmaster. There is, in fact, some evidence that the inexperienced Boyden had been hired to lead Deerfield into oblivion, to "close the Academy for good." The board clearly chose the wrong man for the job, for which we can all be grateful.

Unlike Frank Boyden, you arrive in Deerfield at a decidedly fortunate moment. Deerfield Academy, you will be reassured to hear, is thriving. Moreover, our "ice ages" last a few months, not millennia, our floods rise and fall quickly, and your Deerfield classmates will greet you as friends, not as menu items. Today in Deerfield people from all over the world come here to live and learn together, experiencing a harmony with one another that is utterly at odds with the warring between peoples and cultures that marks this place's past.

Learn all that you can about this village and this valley; there is inspiration in knowing something of the people who came before you. There is also a rootedness that comes from knowing about the place in which you live. You have come here to build a history together. We look forward to your stories becoming a part of Deerfield just as we hope that Deerfield will become a part of you.

*Brian Rosborough gave this talk on June 14, 1997,
at the homecoming for the Classes of 1981-89, hosted by the Science Department.*

BACK TO THE FUTURE

Brian A. Rosborough '58P

WELCOME BACK TO THE FUTURE. When Eric Widmer returned to Deerfield a few years ago, he convened a small meeting of faculty, alumni, and administrators to discuss the Bicentennial and its implications for the school. We imagined a series of celebrations, like this one, bringing clumps of distinguished alumni, like you, back into orbit with the faculty so you could get a sense of this place, what it has meant to your life, the values you hold dearly, and where those values are leading us.

I must not have kept my head down at the meeting. The Headmaster asked me to be provocative on one of these occasions, to talk about the anthropology of Deerfield—who are we, where have we come from, and where are we going, in 35 minutes or less, which left me with a confusion of priorities.

Life is about change over time. How we manage this change has a lot to do with its velocity and our values. While each of us knows a little about the value of time, and as we get older how precious it is, we don't really perceive change over time unless we go back and look at ourselves in a bathing suit, at 16. But the future cometh in a hurry, so let's look at change from where you sit, so we don't just drift through it. To get a running start on the future, I thought I would go back a billion years. Knowing how smart you are, I don't think you will have a problem with this.

In your lifetime we have learned a lot about the cosmic origins of earth, the creation and evolution of our universe and its trajectory through time and space. How little we have made of it. Just in the last year, repairs to the Hubble space craft have given scientists an awesome look into the immensity of deep time, the ability to peer into our past and its prospects for the future. If you imagine one grain of sand, held between your thumb and forefinger at arm's length, that grain of sand, according to recent Hubble photographs, covers 1,500 galaxies as large as ours, stretching for eternities into midnight skies.

If our galaxy were the size of a pea, before the Hubble Deep Field we imagined a pod of peas. Now we see a cathedral of peas (said the Royal Astronomer to the Reverend Peter Gomes of Harvard University). This discovery has brought astronomers to their knees. What can this all mean? All we know is that a lump of matter, the shape of a tennis ball, and theoretically as small as an atom, exploded 15 billion years ago and the debris is still expanding. Hubble II can see back about one third the distance to the leading edge, or 5 billion years ago, during which time our pea, or universe, was formed.

A Deerfield graduate, John McPhee, in his book *Basin and Range*, described this expansive time in terms you and I can understand. If my outstretched hands are 4.5 billion years apart, the age of Earth, everything from my watch to my finger tips represents about a billion years. Your finger tips cover the origin and evolution of all life forms. A single stroke of a nail file would eliminate all human history.

Deerfield Valley, where we sit today, has been through an immense journey from its origins. To give your life a sense of place in time, let's move with this room back a billion years to landscaping on a large scale: the collision of continents, mountain building, earthquakes, lava flows, dinosaurs, formation of lakes, rivers, tributaries, glaciers, native peoples, Puritan settlers, frontiersmen, farmers, and the formation of a school of which you and I are a part.

From whence cometh the hills and the river that were the source of Mr. Boyden's inspiration? To find out, we could drill a core into the 18 mile earth crust, just beneath your seat, into our plate, one of 60, about twice the thickness of the egg shell to the egg, which has been slipping around, diving over and under other plates for a billion years, on its molten mantle mush. Or we could go outside and walk the valleys and river basins, talk with the farmers and the curators in Deerfield's other classrooms. Everything I know about the geo-history of the Connecticut Valley was taught to me by Deerfield's Charlie Danielski yesterday and by Richard Little from Greenfield Community College. I urge you to buy Little's little book, *Dinosaurs, Dunes, and Drifting Continents.* In it he reports:

> 600 million years ago, you were sitting on the Bronson Hill Plate, around Brazil, at 20 degrees south, covered by a warm, shallow sea—surrounded by Brachiopods, mud crawling trilobites, corals, and sea scorpions, 50 million years before sharks and fish swam the ocean. This is

Deerfield. This is bedrock. About 500 million years ago the Bronson Hill Plate crashed into the eastern margin of the Laurentian Plate, crumpling its front fender and forming the Taconic mountains, including the Connecticut River Valley. We rode up over the Laurentian edge, pushing the older rocks of the valley to peaks of 35,000 feet, forming explosive volcanoes.

About 350 million years ago, during the mid-Devonian epoch, when fish began to evolve, we would be sitting right on the equator, which back then divided the US and Canada. Now, the excitement begins. Look out! The Baltica Plate, carrying much of Europe, rams up against Canada and Maine, forming the Arcadian Mountains, or New England Appalachian range. Then the mother of all plates, Gondwana, carrying Africa, South America, India, Antarctica, and Australia, whams into our plate (just where you are sitting), making a big mess.

Like a teenager sliding on a soft rug, these events created a series of folds, or napes, bunching the land up, which backfolded, and over time, with the subterranean heat from these collisions, caused an upward flow of mushy hot rocks which formed gneiss domes and plutons throughout the Connecticut Valley. To the South, the collision formed the Southern Appalachians, from Pennsylvania to Alabama, squeezing the last water out of the Proto-Atlantic Ocean, unifying land into a super continent, called Pangaea, shoving our little valley as high as the Himalayas above sea level and northward to subhumid latitudes.

There we sat for 100 million years, in the mountainous middle of Pangaea, with no action, just eroding away from our 35,000 foot peaks as earthquakes shook the whole contraption so often as to create stretches and cracks. Deerfield was in competition with Boston for the creation of a new ocean. Finally, the crack 150 miles east of Boston won out, causing the same plates to break apart, but this time with North America banging on to the outer edge of Europe and Africa as they set sail for today's Mercator projection, at 1fi inches a year, recreating a 3,000-mile rift and the Atlantic Ocean between us.

For the next 85 million years, the valley eroded, shifted and sank, as sporadic events raised the eastern hills of harder, metamorphic rock. For a while, you were sitting in a big lava lake, 40 miles by 80 miles. From 15,000 to 30,000 feet of adjustment occurred, leaving a lower valley covered with sedimentary rock, an alley of soft stone 50 miles wide and 100 miles long between Northfield and New Haven, laced with rivers flowing west and southwest across fans and alluvial plains into the new Atlantic. Weather and lava flows over millions of years laid down layer upon layer of mud flows, salt flats, and datable soft ash making this valley, above all others on Earth, the world archive of early dinosaur fingerprints discovered in the East. Utah got the bones; we got the prints, 30,000 of them, proving who sauntered, who walked, who ran, and who dragged their tails across our valley floor.

Any ichnologists present? I know you're out there—people with a fetish for footprints. Go directly after lunch to the basement of the Pratt Museum in Amherst and ask to see the print collections of Edward Hitchcock, former Amherst College President and renowned Deerfield master of geology. You will learn more than you think.

Focus for a minute on the most recent 2.5 million years covering 20 ice ages. Just your fingernails. In his book *Global Climate and World Affairs,* Sir Crispin Tickell, an Oxford scholar, now Chairman of Earthwatch Europe, indicates a clear pattern of climate on earth, 150,000 years of cold and ice interrupted by short, 10-15,000 year periods of warmth. All civilizations have occurred in this recent warm patch. While global warming may be rearranging our weather currently, there will be a stack of ice a mile high on this roof in just a few thousand years' time. Count on it.

Now the stage is set for Mr. Boyden's river. These events allowed water courses to cut a path through that alley of soft stone for the mighty Connecticut to reach the sea. The yellow-brown limonite coating on sediment grains was chemically altered to a fine rust-colored redstone which covered every door jamb, church steeple and apartment block from New York to New England in Portland Brownstone through the late 1800s. Deerfield lava cooled and cracked into basalt stone which in time became road and railway beds stretching a thousand miles from where you are sitting.

Millennia of uplift and erosion created and destroyed the valley four or five times. Glaciers robbed inland areas of thick rich top soil, dumping their plunder as far east as Nantucket and the Cape, leaving ten feet of boulders or "till" for two centuries of farmers to harvest into stone walls, a proud heritage reaped from stony ground. In their wake, the melt water left you guys sitting in 400 feet of murky water, for several thousand years, a vast Lake Hitchcock, which extended 150 miles along the Connecticut River to Lyme, New Hampshire.

When the lake drained, 13,000-14,000 years ago, the Connecticut River reappeared, this time out of its ancient, narrow water course, able to meander sensuously across ancient flood plains, or rich alluvial soil, assisted by uplifted lands to the north, released from the weight of ice. New water courses formed, including dramatic drops, like Turner's Falls, forming tight gorges, giving the river enough dance to provide power and to support commerce for Europeans on the distant horizon—including, in time, a lively Headmaster, so nimble and quick.

A billion years in the making—it was as if nature had prepared this place for the *Days of Glory* that were to follow—a wide, verdant valley, with lush soils, ample water, protected by gentler hills, decorated by oxbows and deltas, teeming with wildlife, an alley of prosperity, a river to the seas, God's own sanctuary for teaching and learning about life. Nature designed us and this valley, and did not a bad job of it. We know little of our predecessors, only that the longevity of their cultures is an enduring testament to their skills in adapting to immense changes over time.

Archaeologists say, if early man entered Deerfield Valley earlier than 13,000 years ago, there is no evidence that he brought early woman with him. We think humans came through a corridor in the glacial northeast about 11,500 or 12,500 years ago, at least a thousand years after Lake Hitchcock drained. As the last ice receded, a gradual warming over the last 10,000 years has enabled all civilization, as we know it, to flourish around the world, including life in the Connecticut Valley.

Scientists sort Native Americans in this region in to three periods: paleoIndian, archaic and woodlands. In *The Rise and Fall of an American Indian Nation*, University of Massachusetts archaeologist Dina Dincauze simplified the lifeways of the first New Englanders as pioneers, settlers, and developers, just like us. For about 4,000 years, pioneers, in small bands of hunters and gatherers, roamed about New England. We know little of their culture, language or thought. No human remains have been found in New England, only their trash. Archaeologists will say that about us some day.

It was colder then; the animals were different: mammoth, mastodon, caribou, giant beaver. While the summers warmed, the winters held on. Most pioneers favored coastal settlements, which today are underwater. Deerfield has been inhabited by native Americans for about 300 generations. By 8,000 years ago, elephants were hunted out, caribou driven north, but small game, fish and berries sustained life, until soils deepened and the growing season encouraged the hardy to settle down. No doubt women made this decision. The pioneers must have been geologists, zoologists, and botanists to survive. Today, archaeologists rely on those disciplines and a dozen more climatologists, oceanographers, chemists, engineers, artists, architects—to interpret lost cultures. It keeps us busy. All human civilizations before us have perished.

Six thousand years ago you could still walk from Cape Cod to Martha's Vineyard and Nantucket. The cycles of climate established the cycles of life. People's tools teach us their lifeways. They fashioned food and artifacts from wood, stone and animal skins. By 4,000 B.P. (before the present), they were into the good life; villages were established inland in forest clearings. Division of labor created larger settlements. People stored food, didn't move around as much, and communities, growing in size, required more things for people to do, like ceremonies and fancy burials. The need to maintain good social relationships dictated the size of communal houses, social order, religion and magic.

About 3,000 years ago, the climate cooled, rearranging life in the lowlands. Farming began in earnest about 2,000 B.P. Ceramic vessels replaced older carved soapstone. Labor was mobilized to clear land, plant and harvest crops. The hilling of maize, beans and squash and the use of hoes were common to the region. When conditions were harsh, communal values replaced individual needs. Individual burials ceased in favor of group graves, or ossuaries.

Native Americans knew they were married to nature, and based their value systems on it. Peter Thomas and Bob Paynter, scholars at the University of Massachusetts, speculate about tribal unity prior to European contact. The survival of these cultures must have been due to the egalitarian nature of society, with more cooperation, less competition. Native Americans in segmentary tribes of 300-500 would subdivide in to small bands or families as required by outside pressure. They skillfully used and defended local resources.

When the Puritans stepped ashore, there were eight or ten known villages and perhaps 12,000 Native Americans in the Connecticut Valley, maybe 100,000 native settlers in the New England region, a small part of the tapestry of cultural diversity represented by 2,000 distinct language groups in North America alone. In Meso-America, where the action was, eight to twelve million Native Americans flourished between Brazil and Arizona, reduced to about a million by the end of the Spanish Conquest in 1600.

Devastating plagues, possibly smallpox and other miseries, also decimated the strength of New England populations just after the Puritans landed in the East in the 1630s. Frontier towns reached west, finding open land which our Christian forefathers thought was Divine Providence. Real estate in this village was available in 1665 because the Mohawk had completely wiped out the locals six months before surveyors from Dedham arrived. They staked out an 8,000 acre claim on the velvet-green, soil-rich alluvial plain along the Deerfield River, which they called Pocumtuck after the native peoples who had "abandoned" the site a year earlier.

The Pocumtuck were a proud people, perhaps 500-1200 in all, who co-existed with other Algonkin speaking peoples in the region. Alliances that had existed for hundreds of years with the Iroquois Federation to the north and west were easily exploited by the French-English rivalries that brought competition, commerce, ambition, and western values to the region. The Mohawks were the toughest of this lot, responsible for clearing the land of the Pocumtuck, making Deerfield an easy fetch.

Of course, you all know the history, that the first of three massacres in the fall of 1664 was a skirmish between Indians settling old scores, opening the place for settlement. The second, five miles south of where you are sitting, in September of 1675, was the Bloody Brook massacre which took 60 settlers, including a third of the men in Deerfield. The last, on February 29, 1704, 150 feet away in Historic Deerfield, took 56 lives; 109 or half of the remaining town were captured and marched to Canada, with those surviving being held for ransom. Not surprisingly, many women opted out. Life with the Indians was better than life with the Puritans.

All of this and more is found in a new book called *The Deerfield Reader*, edited by Deerfield's Alan Fraker and Thomas and Karinne Heise, which I heartily recommend. It is the work of our faculty and neighbors, acting in concert to teach history with an interdisciplinary perspective. *A New England Outpost* by our former Dean of Studies, Rick Melvoin, is also a keeper.

As we look to the future, there are some interesting insights that we might take from the founding years and the values of the people who first settled here. Why in the world would you leave the security of Hartford, Springfield and Boston to move to the edge of civilization where drumbeats and hatchets made for sleepless nights? It was not to establish a "city upon a hill," only a village in a valley. This was a different passion from that of first generation settlers and Puritans. The first 200 people who settled in Deerfield were second-generation settlers between 18 and 60 years of age, with a young average age of 35, including 20% widowed or outlawed (some for lascivious or unsociable behavior), half with second spouses.

It was a small, rough crowd, held together with strong, intense Puritan agrarian values, with an indelible sense of order, mission, and tradition. Perhaps Deerfield gave them a sense of place, a mooring to the values they most admired, or had lost. Within five years of founding Deerfield, the Dedham proprietors had not settled. Instead, they sold their shares and released the town to its own independent government. What began as a land deal became much more: a new life, a second chance, a shot at independence, and for some, a fast track to prosperity, not a prosperity measured in wealth, but measured in the pride of coming from a community with enduring values.

The velocity of change suggests the future cometh in a hurry, and it may not be worth what we are going to pay for it. As Ghandi once said: "There must be more to the essence of life than its speed." Without a better understanding of the values and ethics associated with the meaning of life, we stand to miss its tastes and joys. Indeed, we have become progressively proficient about living life, but not any more proficient about understanding its meaning. Like other animals, we must understand the playing field and how it came to be, in order to know how to leave it in playable condition for our children.

After funding 2,000 expeditions, what I have learned can be summed up simply. The mind is happiest when it is learning. Education about how the world works is the best investment we can give to our children and ourselves, and is sure to yield a high return. Most of life is learned outdoors. There is no better capital than human capital.

Perhaps we need to see life differently if we are to pass it on successfully, so others may experience its majesty and cope with its surprises. Deerfield should teach what it means to be alive in the twenty-first century, what it means to be an American, to be a citizen with all its social, political, economic and moral implications. As a people, Americans are said to have a sense of optimism, tempered by a suspicion of authority, with a low regard for whiners, and an unshakable belief in the worth of an individual.

But what is the source of our inspiration? Of our identity? Are we designing a "city upon a hill" or are we passengers outbound in life to destinations unknown, living vicariously, in a dither about what it all means? In truth, the anthropology of Deerfield is the anthropology of humankind. We are villages everywhere, raising children to make choices that are moral, enlightened, selfless, and restorative of life itself. It is the way to the future: who we were, who we are, who we become.

Whether those galaxies, hidden behind your grain of sand, are lifeless or not, rejoice in the possibilities of life ahead, and all that Providence has landed on our shoulders. I take comfort in your collective imagination. Who among you will step forward to lead the immense journey into our uncharted future?

Suzanne Flynt spoke to Deerfield students at their final Bicentennial gathering,
in the Memorial Auditorium, January 17, 1999.
She accompanied her talk with slides from the PVMA collection.

LIFE AT DEERFIELD ACADEMY 200 YEARS AGO

Suzanne L. Flynt

DURING THE PAST TWO YEARS, much has been said and done to celebrate the two hundredth anniversary of the founding of Deerfield Academy. Not surprisingly, the celebration has recognized many significant people who have contributed to the success of this institution. Over the past two hundred years, many students and faculty members have left their footprints in Deerfield. Some of those footprints have survived, and the stories of their owners have been passed down through the years.

Other participants in the founding years have left without a trace. One pupil, Artemas Whitney, did just that. Unfortunately for him, he forgot his copy of *A Grammatical System of the English Language* (Caleb Alexander, 1798) and on the reverse of the title page, Deerfield patriarch Consider Dickinson recorded his faults for posterity: "Artemas Whitney left here for Ashby, in Middlesex, where he belonged; on a visit at Thanksgiving, to get money as he said to pay me for three months board, he hir-d a Horse of Timothy Billings, South Parish. I do not know, but he & the Horse, are a going yet; for he never has returned, or Either of us receivd any compensation." Consider Dickinson's inscription serves as a reminder of human frailties. Although this particular 1799 Academy pupil defaulted on his board payment and stole a horse, this is not the type of story often recorded in histories.

Out of curiosity, I did some sleuth work on Artemas Whitney and learned he was one of 25 children, which perhaps accounted for some lapse in parental guidance about this matter of accountability and morals, and that Artemas was lost at sea with two of his brothers. Not a happy ending. Fortunately, the Academy has survived in good stead despite occasional scoundrels like Artemas Whitney.

What I hope to do in this short presentation is tell you a little about the Academy's early years. Its establishment in 1797 brought about many positive changes to this small agricultural community. Not only did the Academy enable young men and women to attain a secondary education, but it also changed the character of the town so much that in 1799, preceptor Claudius Herrick wrote in a letter to a former Yale classmate: "The Academy is here about what Yale College is at New Haven." These were high aspirations for the fledging academy.

Deerfield Academy, which opened in January 1799, was established for ". . . the promotion of piety, religion, and morality, and for the education of youth in the liberal arts and sciences, and all other useful learning." Qualifications for admission were modest, requiring only that "Youth of both sexes, provided they were found, [were] capable of reading and writing." The inclusion of females was considered important so that not only " . . . the Fathers, but, that the future Mothers of our race, may be richly furnished to train up their children to learning and virtue, and to become the Timothies, and Pauls, the Moseses, and Solomons, of succeeding ages." (This taken from the sermon delivered by Rev. Joseph Lyman at the opening of Deerfield Academy).

Education for young women in the late eighteenth century was advocated by forward-thinking educators, but its desirability was of dubious concern to some young ladies. A play given at a Greenfield school in 1799 had one of the young female characters objecting to attending school, rationalizing that "Uncle Tristam says he hates to have girls go to school, it makes them so dam'd uppish & so deuced proud that they won't work" and "How will the young fellows take it if we shine away & don't like their humdrum ways—won't they be as mad as vengeance—& associate with the girls that don't go to school?" With the prospect of a future confined to household employment, it was of questionable usefulness for many young women to want an advanced education. As books such as the 1799 *Lectures on Female Education* reminded them, "To be obedient daughters, faithful wives, and prudent mothers; to be useful in the affairs of a house; to be sensible companions, and affectionate friends, are, without a doubt, the principal objects of female duty." It was with these often repeated sentiments that fathers dared to send their daughters to be educated at Deerfield Academy.

The founders of Deerfield Academy held great promise in their dream. The Academy building was designed in 1797 by twenty-four year old Asher Benjamin, a journeyman housewright who authored *The Country Builders Assistant,* America's first architectural pattern book, published in Greenfield in 1797. Asher Benjamin lived in the area only a few short years, but during that time he received important commissions, including the ambitious William Coleman house on Bank Row in Greenfield and the Jonathan Leavitt house (now the Greenfield Public Library). Although Asa Stebbins's house in Deerfield was clearly inspired by the Academy building, it is uncertain what Asher Benjamin's role was in its design or execution. The Academy was built as a two-storied neoclassical, brick structure with a hipped roof. Masonry, then used to create elegant, fireproof buildings in large cities, was just beginning to be used in rural areas. The facade was distinguished by two doorways with Gibbsian, or rusticated surrounds, and a slightly projecting beltcourse between the first and second floors. The doors were embellished with semi-circular fan lights. The Asa Stebbins house front doorway gives us a good idea of the original appearance of the Academy's front doors.

Unfortunately, we do not know all the details of the original exterior. A third story was added in 1809, and in 1879, when the Academy was converted into the Pocumtuck Valley Memorial Association's museum, Memorial Hall, the roof was raised yet again. While it is likely that the current roof silhouette closely resembles the original, a balustrade might have graced Asher Benjamin's original design. As well, the early Federal style wood cornice that included a single row of blocks was lost in 1879 when the more elaborate Victorian brick cornice and arched third-floor windows were added. Also, the two front doors were eliminated and the rusticated door surrounds were chiseled off. The right door was bricked in to create a window and the left door was enlarged to accommodate a widened double door.

It is possible that the building originally had shutters, and that the brickwork was painted white or a stone color, which was often done to both enhance a structure's appearance and protect or cover brick of varying quality. Unfortunately, there are many unanswered questions about the appearance of the original Academy. Preceptor Claudius Herrick's 1799 letter also described the interior arrangement and room usage: "The Academy is an elegant Edifice, having, on the lower floor, four rooms, one for the English school, one for the Latin & Greek School, the Preceptor's room and a room for the Museum and Library. The upper room, being all in one, is used for examinations, and exhibitions." Beginning in 1797, curiosities from around the world, along with the important local Native American artifacts, were collected for the Deerfield Academy Museum. About one-third of the original museum survives today in Memorial Hall. Some of the more remarkable artifacts were collected from the Northwest coast.

The school year was divided into four quarters and each quarter lasted eleven or twelve weeks. The concentration of students was males in the winter, and usually females in summer. Academy pupils were usually in their teens, but students as young as ten or as old as thirty were also enrolled. Familial obligations, working on the farm or attending to family needs (whether it be helping with younger siblings or an older, sick family member), took priority over academic ambition. Often the age of a pupil depended more on family circumstances than on aptitude. Rhoda Bardwell of Northfield was 25 years old when she attended the school in 1800.

The health and well being of students and their families was not far from anyone's mind in old Hampshire County during this period. In 1802, a dysentery epidemic pervaded Greenfield and Shelburne, causing respectively 57 and 34 deaths in those towns. During the summer of 1802, Greenfield stores and businesses were almost entirely closed and "Travellers avoided the place as much as possible, and many who passed through town tied mufflers over their faces to prevent inhaling infectious matter." Many families left their homes, and many more sent their children away.

In May of 1803, Elihu and Mercy Bardwell Smead of Shelburne enrolled their twelve-year-old daughter Polly at Deerfield Academy. The privately-owned Smead family register listing the fifteen children of Elihu Smead and his two wives is a sobering reminder of the high mortality rate in many families—only four Smead children lived past the age of eighteen. The Smeads' decision to send their daughter Polly to the Academy was probably one of the worst decisions they made in their lives. Within weeks after Polly began her schooling, the dysentery epidemic broke out in Deerfield, taking the lives of at least 54 people that summer. On July 29, after being in Deerfield less than two months, Polly died. In the following four weeks, three of her siblings also died from this contagious disease. Dr. William Stoddard Williams records in his day book traveling to Shelburne to visit and advise Elihu Smead. But there was little he could do—the medical know-how to stop the intestinal infection was then unavailable.

The prevailing fashion for young ladies—to be accomplished in the ornamental branches of education—prompted many schools in the early nineteenth century to offer instruction in the arts. Deerfield Academy recognized and fostered these tendencies. In 1804, Betsy Mason of Shelburne completed a memorial embroidery to Susanna Paine, and in that same year, 16-year-old Martha Phelps stitched her ambitious embroidery. She began the memorial within a month after her 33-year-old mother died, and dedicated the second monument to her brother Charles.

In 1808, male pupils had the opportunity to take a class in military history and science with Major General Epaphras Hoyt, who served as high sheriff from 1814 to 1831. Among his other books on military science, *Hoyt's*

Practical Instructions for Military Officers, published in Greenfield in 1811, would have served as fodder for the classroom. One illustration informs us "How to Prevent Cavalry Surprises" in the defense of a village.

On the last Tuesday in each quarter, public examinations were held "in the various branches of academic learning" and, twice a year, the students would demonstrate their newly acquired knowledge during a program of "speeches, declamations, dialogues, and orations" attended by parents, trustees, and towns people. Deerfield Academy pupil Elijah Nims and his sister Electa owned the volume *Lessons in Elocution; or, a Selection of Pieces*. Afterwards, pupils and their guests celebrated at the Exhibition Ball.

Pupils were often instructed in cartography, which required a knowledge of geography as well as drawing. A map drawn by Martha Washington Saxton about 1815 of "The world agreeable to the latest discoveries" illustrates her competency in both. Students were advised on the benefits of map making, "Besides the necessity of maps for understanding history, the memory is wonderfully assisted by the local association which they supply. The battles of Issus and Granicus will not be confounded by those who have taken the pains to trace the rivers on whose banks they fought. . . ." (Jedidiah Morse, *Geography Made Easy*, the book Martha Saxton used to draw her map.)

Then, as now, excellence in teaching is what distinguishes better educational institutions. Academy pupils under the tutelage of preceptress Orra White and her future husband, Edward Hitchcock, were fortunate indeed. The "Herbarium, parvum, pictum," which Orra compiled in 1817 and 1818, consists of watercolors of locally collected botanical specimens and was likely used as an aid in botany instruction. She later drew most of the 232 plates and 1,135 wood cuts used to illustrate Edward Hitchcock's scientific publications.

Edward Hitchcock was a Deerfield boy who attended the Academy for six terms. He excelled in the sciences, astronomy and geology being his greatest interests. In 1814, Edward wrote the play *Emancipation of Europe or the Downfall of Bonapart: A Tragedy*, which he later called "a juvenile production which should not have been published. But it contains some real poetry, and was loudly called for by the rural population before whom it was acted with much success." An astronomical apparatus made by Edward Hitchcock to calculate eclipses while he taught at the Academy was responsible for findings which "he entered on a contest with the magnates of astronomical science in the old world, and came off acknowledged conqueror." Hitchcock went on subsequently to become a minister, Professor of Chemistry, Geology, Theology and Natural History, and President of

Amherst College. Hitchcock's six terms as a pupil at Deerfield Academy well prepared him for an impressive career.

While details of the Academy's earliest athletic programs are uncertain, an 1803 copy of *Gymnastics for Youth: or A Practical Guide to Healthful and Amusing Exercises for the Use of Schools* by C.G. Salzmann was owned by the Deerfield Social Library and readily available for scrutiny. As the engraved plates illustrate, bathing and swimming, preservation of equilibrium, climbing and wrestling were just a few of the activities engaged in. Salzmann wrote the book with this in mind: "I have had in view a youth destined to the pursuit of science; and I do not think such a one should ever employ more than nine hours a day in study, and then he will have four left for gymnastic exercises." Nine hours of study, four hours of exercises: does this differ much from today?

It has been two hundred years since the Academy opened. The population of Deerfield has grown from 1,531 inhabitants in 1800 to 5,018 as of 1990. Still it is a small town however you look at it. Technology has gone from a quill pen and ink to a computer; housing has gone from boarding in a spare bedroom in a Deerfield home, where the pupil was expected to contribute to the needs of the household and farm, to state-of-the-art dormitories where every possible need of the student is met. Transportation has evolved from horses and carriages to cars, limousines, buses and planes. Pupils previously learned about the outside world from their geography books. Today you learn about the world from the media, travel, computers, and your international student and faculty population.

While it is said by some that in the olden days students had it harder and that their very survival, from the elements or from disease, was as much a part of their life as what they learned from the books, it would be deceiving to think that life for students is easy today. Times have changed, what students today are expected to know has drastically increased, and what they will accomplish in this world was unimaginable two hundred years ago.

Bob Merriam prepared these remarks for a panel discussion,
"Our School at the Millennium," that was part of
"The School's Program for Our Alumni"
during the Grand Celebration weekend, October 3, 1998.

SCHOOLMASTERING

Robert L. Merriam '43P

FIRST, I WOULD LIKE TO TAKE THIS OPPORTUNITY to thank those who have made possible the Chair in Mary's and my name. When Eric and Meera announced it in June, I was so overwhelmed that I was speechless. So now I thank you. I don't often have a public forum, so I would like to take this opportunity to forgive a few people. First, Bill Lane, who when I was a sophomore threw me out in the snow, because I was bothersome to him. Second, Jim Stevens, who dumped a pail of water on me one night in the dormitory. And, third, Brian Rosborough, who would get the entire corridor up when I returned from courting Mary.

In 1950, Dr. Park at a Baccalaureate turned to Mr. Boyden and said, "It was in 1902, forty-eight years ago, that you first invited me to Deerfield." I gasped to think of the continuity of which they spoke. Now, here it is 1998, and the forty-eight years since 1950 doesn't seem so long. Sometime in the 1950s a Dr. Fellenberg described education as "that which embraces the culture of the whole man with all his faculties, subjecting his senses, understanding and passions to reason, to conscience, and to evangelical laws." And William Ellery Channing said that education is not just a stimulus to learning. Though talent can be worshipped, if it is divorced from rectitude, it will prove more a demon than a benefit.

These statements seem to me to embody what Frank Boyden meant by schoolmastering. And it is my opinion that schoolmastering is what made Deerfield great. Of course, the academic is important, but Frank Boyden's primary interest was to establish a society, morally responsible, community-minded and respectful of others, coupled with learning that would enable the student to make a difference in the world and to accept responsibility. He also believed that authority gives the opportunity to grow beyond yourselves, and he often used horses to interpret his philosophy. "I like a light rein," he said, "but one that can be pulled up tight if necessary." Can you ever forget his "spread-eagle" when the student body questioned a referee or the "open sewer" look when an off-color remark was made?

One of the great teachers was Red Sullivan. He combined a deep understanding of boys and a willingness to pull them up quickly when it was necessary. In his second year at Deerfield, Red decided that he would reason with his students and have long heart-to-hearts with them. After a few weeks of this, the boys came to him one evening and said "Mr. Sullivan, would you please just hit us instead of these lecture sessions?" None of you, I am sure, who were under his tutelage in the John Williams House will forget your late evening runs around the lower level, designed to wear off your excess energy.

Some of you remember Beaver Smith. How we hated those 2:10 meetings Sunday afternoon when the meeting was prolonged for Mr. Smith to tell another story. We heard the same story year after year. You remember it. There was a drunk on the train who asked the conductor how many days there were between Christmas and New Year's. "Seven," says the conductor. "Then," says the drunk, "how many between New Year's and Christmas?" "Seven," says the conductor. "No," says the drunk, "there are three hundred and fifty eight." Then we would all cheer and clap and Mr. Smith would be pleased and Mr. Boyden would thank us for listening.

It's not really in keeping with the subject today, but you might like to know that Mr. Smith was well known for his punctuality. He was asked to speak to the Ladies' Garden Club at 8:00. When 8:00 arrived, he was the only one in the room, but he rose anyway and began to deliver his talk. The ladies were taught a good lesson.

Part of Frank Boyden's philosophy was not to take yourself too seriously, and he sometimes told stories about himself. During the summer, he would sit on the back porch of the Ephraim Williams House hoping that someone would come by, so that he could talk about the school. One afternoon after he had showed two ladies through the John Williams House, they offered him a tip and said they heard there was an interesting man running the school. "Did he ever see him?" they asked. "Oh yes, 'most every day." "Do you like him?" "Oh yes, very much," he replied.

One summer he and Claude Allen, the headmaster of Hebron, were in Camden, Maine. Claude was a pontifical sort of a person, what one thinks about as the typical headmaster. One of the old timers loafing on the dock turned to his friend and said, "I hear that is the headmaster of Deerfield Academy." "Oh," said the friend, "who is the little guy with him?"

After the boys had gone to bed, the switchboard was plugged into the phone by the Boydens' bed. One night shortly after I had joined the faculty, Walter Fisher called, and when the phone was answered, Walter, thinking it was me, said, "Hey squirt, how are you." "Oh," said Mr. Boyden, "hello, Walter. I am fine, how are you?"

Deerfield never had a catalogue and a list of rules, for the only rule was to be a gentleman. It was the same rule that Robert E. Lee had at Washington and Lee. Now I know that would be impossible today, but it did make it possible to make exceptions when rules needed to be broken.

Above all, the faculty at Deerfield were expected to be on hand for every activity when school was in session. There was a singleness of purpose for everyone at Deerfield. The students were expected to devote themselves to their work; the faculty and the staff to schoolmastering. For Frank Boyden that singleness of purpose was every day of the year. Harold Dodd of Princeton and Lewis Perry of Exeter always told the story of visiting Mr. Boyden at the Breakers in Palm Beach, where they found him reading *The Pocumtuck.*

Every detail of a boy's life at Deerfield was considered. Planning was important. In 1943, a group of us were to be in Boston for the Navy V-12 program physicals and interviews. The night before, we were lined up in the school building hall. Mr. Boyden was at his desk. When our name was called, we walked to the desk, and shook hands with the Headmaster. He sat down to sign letters. We were to stand at attention until he motioned us to sit. As soon as we did, he pushed a pencil onto the floor to see if we reacted quickly to pick it up. If we didn't meet his criteria, we were sent back to practice again. The next day in Boston each of us was greeted by a naval officer who did exactly the same thing.

I wonder how many of you know why you were assigned particular rooms in a corridor. If you were a good boy, you could have the room at the end of the corridor. If you were questionable, you were closer to the corridor master. Deerfield has always given close attention to details. Just take a look at the planning for this event. Many can remember practicing marching so we would look good marching to a football game. That planning went into everything at the Academy. When a trustee once said the oyster stew was excellent, oyster stew was served at every trustees' luncheon from then on.

Of course, I can tell you stories of my own teaching in the classroom, on the field, in the dining room, the dormitory and every other location, but two incidents will suffice. The first evening of the school year, Mr. Boyden and I met the first ten boys on the new boy list so that they could practice standing straight and tall and saying "here" clearly when their feet were firmly planted on the floor. The theory was if they did it well, all would try to emulate them. There was a basic trust that there was good in every boy. Many of you have heard the statement, "We don't do that at Deerfield. I am putting my trust in you that it will not occur again."

One morning at 3:00 a.m. I drove Mr. Boyden to a little town south of Deerfield to meet the police, who had picked up one of our students who had borrowed a local car. The boy was turned over to us, brought back to school and told to go to bed but to be sure to be at breakfast on time and the next day to call on the automobile owner to apologize. No one else ever knew of the incident, but the boy knew he had been wrong and his loyalty to the Headmaster was firm.

Teaching was what I was taught and I taught what I was taught. Of course, times have changed and the school, just like our society, has changed, but Deerfield still teaches respect for others and has an expectation that the students will be ladies and gentlemen. I am sure there is much good schoolmastering at Deerfield today. I know of two instances: one, when the Headmaster met with a very fine student musician who was upset when she missed a note at the Baccalaureate; the other, when the faculty were advised it was important that each and every one feel an obligation to speak to students if they simply rose from the table without excusing themselves or when they wore their caps in the dining room or in the classroom. The amenities are a part of schoolmastering and are taught at Deerfield.

What I have tried to say is that the teaching experience is a learning experience. Hopefully, what I learned from students, faculty and staff enabled me to be a schoolmaster.

*This panel discussion took place on September 12, 1997,
as part of the homecoming program for the Classes of 1912-1947,
hosted by the Mathematics Department.
Students with an interest in careers in medicine attended the program.*

MEDICAL PRACTICE: WHAT'S NEW, WHAT'S NOT

*Paul Didisheim, M.D. '45, Kendrick P. Lance, M.D. '45,
Robert E. McCabe, Jr. M.D. '44, Edwin P. Maynard, M.D. '44P*

Kendrick P. Lance, M.D. '45, Moderator. We have three randomly chosen international players who are in the forefront of their field, and one
regional player who knows how things are in north New Jersey, that's me.
We will range from a discussion of George Washington's wooden teeth to
comments on the percent of gross national product expended annually on
health care. Our first speaker is Paul Didisheim. If we all threw our curricu-
la vitae down the stairway, his, by far the heaviest, would hit bottom first.
Paul will speak on aspects of tissue engineering.

Paul Didisheim, M.D. '45. First of all, I would like to pass this device
around among the students in the second row. I do need it back, though.
Some patient is waiting for it. This is a Jarvik 5 total artificial heart. It is
held together by Velcro and rubber bands. The Velcro is real, and it keeps
the two sides of the heart together. The rubber bands are my addition, to
keep it from falling apart during the trip. This particular one was developed
about 20 years ago, and there have been major improvements since then,
through a program funded by the National Heart, Lung, and Blood
Institute. Still there isn't a device which is satisfactory for implantation in
human patients, principally because of thrombosis, blood clotting as well as
infections that occur when these devices are implanted.

Believe it or not, when I was at Deerfield, I wanted to be a poet. In
fact, I published a couple of poems in *The Scroll*, along with our classmate
John Ashbery. The only difference between him and me is that he went on
to get a Pulitzer Prize for poetry, and my career as a poet was snuffed out in
my freshman year at Princeton by my English professor. Lack of creativity, he
said, so I went on to become a doctor.

My interest in medicine, particularly the problems with blood clotting, came from my grandparents' strokes. Most people have strokes when they reach the ages of 80 and 90, as my grandparents did. It is a prevalent condition, for which there is still not an adequate preventive measure.

At Johns Hopkins I took the opportunity to do a little research during my second year, became enamored of the career and have been doing, managing, administering or fostering it my entire professional life. The nice thing about medicine is that you can do all sorts of different things: you can practice, you can teach, you can do research, you can administer, you can travel quite a bit. Despite the fact that it has become more and more of a business and less and less of a calling, I still think that it is one of the most significant things one can do with one's life.

§.

[Dr. Didisheim showed a slide with each of the following remarks.]

—The National Institutes of Health. Here we really do have the opportunity to make a difference on a national scale. NIH is the largest biomedical research facility in the world, with a 13 billion dollar annual budget. Our institute, the National Heart, Lung and Blood Institute, has a 1.3 billion dollar annual budget, larger that that of a lot of small countries. Incredibly, it has not been enough to conquer heart disease, stroke, cancer, and AIDS, the principal causes of death and illness in the country today

—An early artificial heart valve, made of titanium, stainless steel and plastics, introduced about 40 years ago.

—A more modern heart valve. Because of careful engineering, the flow through these valves has been markedly improved, and the incidence of clotting and stroke has been reduced but by no means eliminated. 40-50,000 of these devices are implanted every year in this country, but a certain degree of clotting continues to occur because the blood is changed by its contact with foreign surfaces. Some of you sitting in the second row will no doubt solve this problem.

—Another kind of heart valve, made out of animal tissues, from pig heart valves or cow heart coverings or pericardium. The animal tissue has been treated so as to prevent antibody reaction. It does not cause clotting because it is closer to human tissue, but it does disintegrate or calcify after a dozen or so years.

—A ventricular assist system. Here the original heart is still in place and the blood is taken from the heart and pumped through this pump and then back into the heart so as to give it a boost. Several thousand patients around the world now have these.

—Tissue engineering. Tissue engineering marries the discipline of engineering with the science of molecular and cellular biology, to produce an assembly of functional tissues and organs from native or synthetic sources. This is a new interdisciplinary field of the last decade and is taking hold in cardiovascular disease, where new types of devices originate from human cells and therefore will not be responded to as foreign.

—Controlled drug release. These little wafers are filled with chemotherapy agents and then implanted into the brains of patients with brain cancer. Studies have recently shown marked improvement and prolonged life. This reminds me of our fellow undergraduate, John Gunther, who died of brain cancer in 1945 and whose father wrote the book *Death Be Not Proud* about him. Had this treatment been available then, he might be alive today.

This has been a brief adventure through various aspects of medical research. The profession needs young people like you, and I hope you seriously consider entering it.

Lance. Bob McCabe holds a position of preeminence in the field of kidney transplantation and also organ preservation. He has been interested in body parts and will speak to us on that topic.

Robert E. McCabe, Jr. M.D. '44 . Early in my internship, a friend of mine, Al Mead at the New York Hospital, came to me and asked me as a surgical intern to hook a patient dying of acute renal failure up to a machine he called Kolff's washtub. It looked very much like an old Maytag washing machine. Needless to say, our patient died and we thought our medical careers would come to an end when our chiefs heard about our experiment. But dialysis did take off, and the beginning of transplantation was dependent on the dialysis machine. However, none of the artificial organs are ever as good as the primary organ, so there is always a role for transplantation therapy.

Man has always been interested in transplantation, from the ancient Greeks' chimera, who was a she-goat with the head of a lion and tail of a dragon, to a Renaissance painting by Fra Angelico, depicting a clergyman dying of cancer, on whom they had transplanted the leg of a dead patient. The first clinical experiments in transplantation were blood transfusions, and then skin grafts to treat the burns of soldiers during World War II. The rejection of these grafts demonstrated a sophisticated and complex system of immune defenses which we had to learn to combat chemotherapeutically for transplant surgery. Because of the knowledge about skin allografts thereafter and the knowledge that identical twins had the same immunological make-up, Dr. Joseph Murray performed the first twin transplant, an isograft (meaning that the tissue was from an immunologically identical source).

I remained far more interested in the clinical, technical and mechanical aspects of transplantation because I was trained in vascular surgery. The kidney is a privileged organ for transplantation for two reasons. First, we have a machine to keep the patient alive, and second it is a paired organ. As my friend Sam Koontz said, "God gave us two kidneys so surgeons could transplant one of them."

We needed to change a number of factors in those days in order to have an effective referral system to get the material needed for transplants. First of all, we had to redefine death to include what is now commonly known as brain death. Then we launched the donor card program, an educational program for the public about organ transplantation, to encourage people to give us permission to use organs. As a consequence, we established the New England Organ Bank in Boston and the Regional Transplant Program in New York City. All this led to the United Network of Organ Sharing, which has now put the whole system on a national basis. We had to get the medical examiners behind this and convince them that brain death was legal death.

But before any of this was really possible, we had to have a means for preserving the organs. We would chill the organ down to four degrees centigrade, with special solutions, and we developed techniques so that we can now preserve a kidney for 24-48 hours, the liver a comparable length of time. The kidney machine was a very important instrument in promoting broad-based kidney sharing, not only across the United States but to Europe and Russia. For the heart and liver, much more complicated organs, we have not been able to find a comparable machine.

I got involved in transplantation because we had the first of these kidney machines in New York City. Being the youngest person on the staff, I was told to go learn how to use it. Looking for an opportunity to make a name for myself, I grabbed the ball and made a professional career out of studying organ preservation. In spite of the many developments, there are currently 53,000 patients awaiting transplant in the US, the majority of these waiting for a kidney.

Have we gone too far? Not yet. Will xenografts take us too far? They might. Maybe we can change the pig heart so that we can use all, not just a part, of it in whole organ transplantation. These are ethical issues. Genetic engineering may be the answer to the xenograft barrier, which is far more difficult to overcome than the allograft barrier. Is it feasible? Yes. Economical? Probably. Frightening? Maybe. Will such achievements be acceptable? Only time will tell, but maybe someday we will create a true Frankensteinian monster, with the brain of Einstein, the heart of a lion and the longevity of Methuselah.

Lance. Ed Maynard is an eminent person in the delivery of health care and health care issues.

Edwin P. Maynard, M.D. '44P . With the control or elimination of a number of diseases in the past 50 years, has come a tremendous change in the scope and complexity of our health care endeavor. All of it has been beneficial but has come at great cost. In the 1940s when we were at Deerfield, health care in the US consumed perhaps 1-2% of our economy. Health care costs have screamed up well beyond the percentage rise in Deerfield's tuition, to the point where we now consume about 15% of our GNP on health.

Along with this have come changes in administration and finance. For example, when I first came to the MGH we were essentially a charity institution delivering free care or charging modest fees. For people in the moderate income group, the day rate at the hospital was $15, a far cry from the figure of over $1,000 per day at this time. The first response to this of course was to bring in insurance. The money was there so prices continued to zoom upwards. Then in the 1970s, industry, which had picked up health insurance for employees, rebelled. That move led to the dominant theme of cost containment in United States health care today. Our society has decided that we can no longer afford everything for everybody and that we have to ration our health care.

The next response to industry's cry was the development of various managed care programs, the purpose of which is to set up a series of barriers, to hospitalization, technologies, physician referrals to specialists, or even drugs. The most recent trend is toward prepayment, which shifts the incentive for cost containment to the providers. This too has ethical problems, when hospitals and physicians have to say that they must limit their services.

What can we project for the future? First, we have to admit that our system is not ideal, with 15% of our population without insurance and a larger percentage grossly underinsured. Also, we need to understand that the pattern of health care change in our country is incremental. We tend not to make major leaps. I am convinced that before long we will decide that universal health insurance for our entire population is not only morally obligatory but also essential and beneficial for our country. We remain the only industrialized country in the western world that does not offer universal health care to its population. Meanwhile, medicine remains an extremely attractive profession. We are still getting a goodly share of the best and the brightest, including able Deerfield graduates. As for me personally, I am still happy to go to the hospital in the morning and see my patients with their challenging problems, and I love to go over to the medical school and meet the students.

Lance. The attraction to medicine is science or caring or both. Medicine is a calling, not a job. Essentially medical practice is an exercise in humanity, with person to person interchange between doctor and patients, who freely grant the physician full access to their problems, innermost thoughts and even their bodies. This relationship requires mutual trust and involves considerable risk to both parties. Such a fragile shared understanding between a stressed patient and a supportive physician is not at all implicit in a business arrangement between a provider and the consumer. Many have expressed a warning that the physician cannot both be a fully committed advocate for the patient while also functioning as the employee of a cost-focused business, which primarily exists to generate profit. Recent events clearly illuminate this conflict of interest, and changes are beginning to appear.

It is a wonderful and awful thing to look back on 50 years of medical care and realize how quickly it goes, how little time since we left those front seats here, looking forward to our careers, to now, when we look back and see where we have been, to where the successes and failures have been. In a medical career the successes are many and the failures haunt you forever.

Main School Building, Deerfield

Photograph - Bob Bliss, 1956
The Pocumtuck
Deerfield Academy Archives
Deerfield, Massachusetts

III. "A COMMUNITY OF INTERPRETATION."

Arthur J. Clement '66 spoke at the Homecoming for the Classes of 1960-1968, hosted by the English Department on April 18, 1997. In his talk, "The Teacher is Father to the Child," he eloquently remembered his English teacher, Mo Hunt, and how that "gracious spirit" introduced him to "a new vision of inclusion" through the readings assigned in the course. This section of the anthology, focusing on teaching, takes its title from Arthur's statement, "Deerfield is more than a residential community; it is a community of interpretation."

Frank Henry spoke in a panel discussion, "Our School at the Millennium,"
part of "The School's Program for Our Alumni,"
during the Grand Celebration Weekend, October 3, 1998.

KEEPING THE WATCH

Frank C. Henry, Jr. '69

BY IMPLICATION, BOB MERRIAM has reminded us that Deerfield was vulnerable on February 28, 1704, because, as George Sheldon said, the watch was unfaithful. I assert, as would, I think, Bob, that the watch today is kept by the faculty.

One afternoon in November 1988, during an English III class while we were trying to unravel Emerson's "Self-Reliance," a boy from North Carolina, one of those fellows who sincerely refers to the altercation in the 1860s as the War of Northern Aggression, stopped the class and asked, "Who picks the books we read?" I allowed that the teachers of English III select some books together, but we each made our own choices in the end. During a long pause he contemplated me and my answer and finally concluded, "You are a very powerful man." I don't know if I had ever realized before then the gravity of his observation, but now I never forget it.

I am not certain whether the world is rapidly changing in new or fundamental ways, or if it is simply changing as it always has. I do know that at Deerfield the means of teaching are changing, but the outcomes are no more predictable for us than they were for the first principal, Enos Bronson, in 1799, or Virgil Howard, the principal during the Civil War and the second longest serving head of school, or Frank Boyden. Part of my credo, though, is that teachers make a difference in the lives of young people. I know the irreversible influence that Bob McGlynn had on me when I took up my independent work in college, chose my graduate education, and redirected my career. Moments occur in class when I watch myself and realize I am manifesting BVL [Bryce Lambert] characteristics. I don't have a "very" cutter but I religiously scratch it out.

Teaching students not to use "very" as a common adverb does not assert the enduring values that graduates will need to meet the world's, the country's, and their own needs. But if a student does learn to hesitate before taking the easy, familiar path and instead searches for a more precise, a more accurate adjective or adverb, an enduring truth has been implemented. The student has learned to respect her language as a powerful tool, and just as a carpenter keeps her tools clean and sharp, so too a writer must do the same. In English, mathematics, science, foreign language, and philosophy classes and in fine arts studios, students are challenged daily to sharpen and improve their intellectual tools. Whether it was Daddy Bogues, who taught English from 1928 to 1955, making Thomas Macaulay's "A Piece of Chalk" his text for six months; or Bart Boyden in the 40s, 50s and early 60s with those daily paragraphs chalked on the board; or Leslie Byrnes, history instructor in the tough days of the late 60s and early 70s refusing to accept term papers because the Ibids were not underlined; or now Claudia Lyons chattering, chiding, and chivvying students to produce fluid and fluent French and Kim Wright demanding that students purge the passive from their papers, teachers at Deerfield did, do, and will persist in training students to refine their abilities to read accurately, think carefully and write precisely.

After my father told me about reading "A Piece of Chalk" for months on end, I turned to a reference book to see who Macaulay was, since I had never read, certainly not at Deerfield, a sentence by him. In Margaret Drabble's *Fifth Edition of The Oxford Companion to English Literature* I found Thomas Babbington Macaulay, 1800-1859. She characterizes his *Essays Critical and Historical* as "dogmatic, overbearing, and irredeemably shallow. Lord Acton called them 'A key to half the prejudices of our age'; but their urgent, declamatory style, their bustling self-confidence and biting wit, endeared them to the reading public all over the world." No doubt in 1941 after the fall of France and the feisty air defense of Britain, Daddy Bogues responded warmly to the urgent, declamatory style and the self-confidence when he assigned "A Piece of Chalk" as a model essay.

Many may recall the magician's delight that Larry Haynes, a physics teacher who taught from 1937 till 1971, brought to the demonstration of a triple point, a set of unique conditions under which matter exists simultaneously as a gas, fluid, and solid, as he reduced the atmospheric pressure in a vacuum chamber where a beaker of water boiled and froze all at once. Today, students in physics and chemistry labs never see that demonstration but do manipulate exquisitely accurate probes and record trials on video tape to measure more accurately the force of gravity on mass. In 1942, my father spent a year reading essays. I recall reading with McGlynn in 1968 D.H.

Lawrence's passionate novel of generational tension, *Sons and Lovers,* while a few years later my brother read enough Robert Frost with Merriam to think Frowner was Frost. Today we read little Frost and no Lawrence or Macaulay, but all juniors do read *Their Eyes Were Watching God* by an African-American woman, Zora Neale Hurston. Microsoft Word handles all those pesky footnote problems on term papers. Slide-rules provoke mirth, while programmable, graphing calculators make the Algebra class I took with Peter Hindle seem medieval.

The teacher in 1942 and in 1968 faced widely different worlds than we do today. In 1942, teachers instructed mostly boys, most of whom would serve their country in a contest to which the outcome was unclear but the cause indisputable. In 1968, teachers graduated boys who faced an angry, schismatic society, an ambiguous war, and nebulous mores. Our present context is sitting among classes that are evenly mixed between boys and girls, variously assembled across races, nationalities, and religions and facing a future marked by AIDS, a roller-coaster world economy, an information explosion, terrorists possessing weapons of mass destruction, and accelerating environmental deterioration. Students today consult Spanish, German, and French newspapers on the Internet in their rooms, and arrange terms abroad in China, Botswana, South Africa, Spain, France, or even Damariscotta, Maine. Every year in June dozens of students head off to Europe, not for the grand tour but for further language study and home stays. And within the classrooms teachers are still exercising the power that my young southern gentleman wisely perceived.

For instance, in a junior level class we contemplate John Winthrop's "Model of Christian Charity," consider Crevecoeur's answer to "What is an American?" and carefully parse Jefferson's "Declaration of Independence." We subject the postulates to tests, however, and also read slave narratives from the 1830s, examine the photographs of Jacob Riis, read Tim O'Brien's disorienting short stories about Vietnam, and finally end up with Alex Kotlowitz's *There Are No Children Here*, the documentation of two brothers growing up just west of Chicago in Henry Horner Homes. Students are faced with this question: if Jefferson is correct in the Declaration, do Lafayette and Pharoah Rivers, a pair of African American boys in the late 1980s, have a right, nay a duty, to revolt? Or does John Winthrop have advice for our engagement with those boys? In choosing to make these assignments, we are responding to the world that we see, but we cannot see around the corner; neither could Daddy Bogues or Bob McGlynn.

The means and materials of education clearly change from cultural age to cultural age, each one trying to address the questions that appear to be pertinent. But running through it all, from Mr. Boyden's first days to Eric Widmer's most recent week, the aims have been consistent. In an academy that arose out of the democratic impulses of the Commonwealth and has persisted two hundred years as a secular school, we have and continue to foster a civil society marked by respect for individuality and subordination of one's liberty to the good of the whole. Over time, the number and variety of people who are trying to arrange and live within that civil society has grown. Today 598 students come from 37 states and 18 countries. Arriving at a civil society has grown more difficult but is more rewarding when achieved. And to make that society we must listen to each other carefully, express ourselves thoughtfully, and declare our commitments precisely. The very skills that we hope to cultivate in the classroom are those that are in most demand when fulfilling a social contract.

Deerfield teaches students how to keep the tools of their disciplines sharp and clean, to be familiar with and enthusiastic about the literature of their age, and to believe in and to promote a rational, humanistic society. In 1942, 1968, and 1998, teachers did and do train and persuade their students that discoursing rationally, paying attention to others, and learning to express oneself logically are crucial to a life worth living, and themselves practice that same faith.

As I look at the alumni my father's age and my own age, and then turn to my students, I am struck that what Deerfield has done in the twentieth century and intends to do into the twenty-first is assemble students with above average and often superior ability who are predisposed to work hard and have imagined clear and ambitious goals for themselves, fling them together with teachers of the same qualifications and exhort them to do the best they can with extraordinary resources and limited time. In moments of abbreviation I have called Deerfield a bunch of old overachievers teaching a bunch of overachieving kids. We are a community of great diversity but we all practice secular Puritanism. We work hard and believe that our work will redeem us.

Last night, Peter Fallon offered a reading for the faithful:

Rejoice
in the prudence of a place as it extols

the election of a spirit to grow
instead of wilt . . .

Time weaves loose threads into a pattern.
The ghosts of Charter Day, they are not taciturn;
they resonate and revel
in their legacy, a promise which unfurled
like the flag of liberty. That promise kept.
It said there are uncarved commandments to accept.
Be worthy of this life. And, Love the world.

*At the homecoming for the classes of 1912-1947 on September 13, 1997,
hosted by the Mathematics Department, Wanda Henry, Department Chair,
presented passages she had selected from Mrs. Boyden's letters and sayings.
She drew chiefly on two sources: Mrs. Boyden's contributions to* Deerfield Magazine,
which were written as letters to alumni; and a miniature book, Helen C. Boyden, *by Robert
Merriam, one of a series of such books he created on women of Deerfield.*

HELEN CHILDS BOYDEN

collected by Wanda S. Henry

IT WAS THE YEAR 1902 and I was in college when I heard that a young
Amherst student was coming to be the head of our turbulent Academy.
The school had become the despair of the townspeople—no college
preparatory work was being done—the membership had dwindled to thirteen students. The new Headmaster was much discussed at the Country
Store. One old man said, "It won't take those boys long to run that little
fellow out of school!" But another answered, "You just can't tell by the
looks of a frog how far he'll jump." That was my introduction to your
Headmaster.

Five years later we were married. How well I remember that day.
In the evening, the guests went from Wapping, my home two miles below
Deerfield, to the wedding at the Brick Church in a specially chartered trol-
ley car—and we started our wedding journey in an automobile, the first I'd
ever ridden in. Those first years were years of struggle for us personally and
for the school—but the faith and courage of your Headmaster never
wavered—neither when he had to eat my soggy biscuits, nor when there
wasn't money enough to get good teachers.

Each year the school was a little better than the year before. When
the Old Dormitory was built, and the Headmaster heard me tell someone,
"Here we'll have thirty-five students," he said, "Don't say that—we can't
possibly get that number." But we did—and more—and so the years went
on—and now we have the school as it is today. The frog has jumped a long
way. And you were there. You helped build the school, and now your sons
are carrying on. To them we pass the torch and they will keep the faith,

and year after year, the school will go on and continue to be the school you helped build and the one you dreamed it should be.

§

As to Mr. Boyden, he had a very unhumorous background. I am a Unitarian, and he is a Congregationalist. I think his family would have preferred that he marry a Buddhist.

§

Sayings and mottoes: Don't put numbers into formulas and turn the crank for answers. Learn the fundamentals and then think your way to the answer—They can because they think they can.—Make up your mind what you want in life. Be sure it is worthy; be willing to pay the price; and go get it.—When will you stop trying to remember and start trying to think?—I don't like pictures. They show what I look like.—The sins we commit two by two, we pay for one by one.—The trouble you don't get into you don't have to get out of.—The man who is too big for a small job is too small for a big job.—The difficult we do immediately; the impossible will take a little longer.—You always have to sacrifice something little for something big.

§

As we look at our present gymnasium, it is hard to understand how proud we were of the Barn, but we had just given up a basketball floor located in the assembly hall of the old Academy where, during the games, the students sat on a small stage which protruded well into the court. On one side, to support the ceiling, stood posts which were a constant danger to life and limb of the players. Baskets were often made by shooting over the rafters, a challenge to any visiting team. After that, the Barn seemed palatial. To be sure, when bleachers were put up all across the south side, the playing space became a bit limited. The scorer often watched the game seated on one of the cross beams. The smaller members of the student body and town children lay prone on their stomachs under the bleachers, peeping through upper classmates' legs with their heads cradled in their arms. They looked strangely like the cherubs at the feet of the Sistine Madonna.

§

We had many instructive lectures on Saturday night—travel talks with stereopticon lantern slides, discussions on liquid air, and a thrilling one on "The Life and Growth of the Pea." We all had our minds improved regularly once a week. Then the great day came when Budd Schulberg's father presented us with our first movie projector. Here, also, the audience soon outgrew the seating space. Many a boy will never see Donald Duck without feeling, in memory, some other boy's knees in his back almost pushing him off the bleachers. There was never a chance for any boy's being lonely there. Now we watch our movies in perfect comfort in the new Memorial Building. Will the boys who have never experienced the crowded bleachers of the Barn be able to enjoy those new seats with our enthusiasm?

§

But what would all this have been without the exciting joy of life with you boys? I cherish each familiar scene. In the early morning I see you running late to breakfast, coats unbuttoned and ties untied. Then the clang of the school bell, and boys with precarious piles of books and papers hurrying to homerooms from all directions. And again there you are, sitting in front of me in the classroom—so many now—looking up with faces very like those I taught not too long ago.

It is fall now, and I have the old perplexing problem: which one will answer to the call of John and which to Peter? Will I ever get it straight? But the work will go on in its old familiar pattern. This week we have been pursuing the elusive "mole" and the obscure "22.4." Soon there will be those special drill classes and sharp raps on the knuckles for failure to know the proper valence. When winter comes, we will struggle again with the mysteries of dynamic equilibrium, but the classic snowball fight will make it crystal clear. Then before we know it, spring is here again with its tracery of green leaves and the glorious game of baseball. And another year has gone.

§

Yesterday I walked into my first class of the new year and began reading off the names. How familiar, how pleasant it all was! There were many new names, but in the boys' faces I saw again that same eagerness I remember in yours. There were also many names I have often read before: your brothers'. How glad I am to have them. No matter how brilliant they are, I shall always remember you as good or better. It is well that time leaves always pleasant memories. But not all these were brothers; this year there are your sons, too. How young it made me feel as I thought of you as you sat there struggling over chemical formulas. They will probably do better work than you ever did, but I'll never tell them so.

§

As for me, I struggle happily with "oxidation and reduction," "quadratic equations" and those mysterious "conic sections." In the early morning while the school sleeps, I tend my greenhouse. In the evening when there are not too many papers to correct, I lose a rubber or two of bridge or follow on the television the misadventures of Lucy, whom I dearly love. When the spring comes, there are ball games to watch, and, grieving at the loss of the Braves to Milwaukee, I find solace in watching Jimmie Piersall make phenomenal catches at Fenway Park. And now once more I send you greeting and repeat the wish that I have made for you so often, that happiness and success may come to you all—but that it may never be a low success—and that if at times it must be a failure, let it be a high failure!

§

Always the same story with the same happy ending. Each year we fought the battle of science—hydrogen, oxygen, you and I. We fought against powerful enemies: ignorance, indifference, artistic superiority—against explosions, burst water pipes, the lure of gum, and of longing glances at watches—even one solitary tack strategically placed! Against all of these enemies and even more, we have waged battle in pursuit of truth and come out through college boards and final examinations with banners flying.

§

The real climax of my peaceful summer was when the Hubbards came to visit us. The first thing that happened was that the motor of the dishwasher burned out. Then the oven door of our stove fell off. Last and most tragic calamity, the drain clogged and we could use no water. The next week the cook left and who could blame her? I became once more a cook. I relearned to make bread as good as the loaves my mother used to bake. So you see, as I have so often told you, there are few situations so difficult that they do not yield to repeated attacks of the ordinary mind. Although this summer has been interesting and has developed my ingenuity, happily I go back to the blessed peace of the classroom where, if things go wrong with the mechanisms of the laboratory, Mr. Biddle or Mr. Bohrer will fix them, where I won't have to cook, and where nothing untoward happens to quadratic equations or conic sections.

§

Mr. Boyden told John McPhee: "She is much more important than I am. She has a wonderful sense of humor and deep affection for the boys. She has more influence on the boys than I have. She makes them want to do the work. Her judgment is excellent. It is interesting that a combination such as the two of us could get together. I don't know that I've ever known her, really. She could have been the head of any school."

In awarding her an honorary degree, Smith College said: "To Helen Childs Boyden, who, with some small help from her husband, has built a great school."

John O'Brien gave this talk on April 19, 1997,
at the homecoming for the classes of 1960-1968,
hosted by the English Department.

"THE CHILD IS FATHER OF THE MAN"

John C. O'Brien P'87, '91, '92

UPON HEARING THE TITLE OF ART CLEMENT'S SPEECH FOR TODAY—"The Teacher is Father to the Child"—I was prompted to return to the source of his allusion to find out what the great Romantic nature poet Wordsworth might suggest by way of inspiration for my own talk on the evolution of English instruction at Deerfield over the past thirty years. The poem from which Arthur drew his allusion is entitled, "My Heart Leaps Up When I Behold":

> My heart leaps up when I behold
> A rainbow in the sky:
> So was it when my life began.
> So is it now I am a man.
> So be it when I shall grow old,
> Or let me die!
> The Child is father of the Man;
> And I could wish my days to be
> Bound each to each in natural piety.

Perhaps propitiously, this poem was included in Wordsworth's famous collection, *Lyrical Ballads*, and shares a sort of kinship with our bicentennial purposes here today. Published originally in 1798, a year after the founding of Deerfield Academy, *Lyrical Ballads* celebrated, among other things, the vitality of the imagination, the resiliency of the human spirit, the efficacy of nature, and the wisdom of youth. Indeed, from Wordsworth's memorable lyric we may infer a philosophy of learning that may well have been on the minds of our founders as they wrote the charter for "an Academy in the town of Deerfield" in 1797.

At all events, Wordsworth's philosophy most certainly would have informed the teaching of Mo Hunt in 1967. One of Mo's most endearing qualities at Deerfield was his youthful spirit; whether coaching track, riding his green Raleigh bicycle long and hard around the valley, or engaging students in literary discussion, Mo always projected a childlike enthusiasm for the new, the possible, in books and in boys. It may indeed be true that "the teacher is the father to the child," but as a teacher, I must also agree with Wordsworth, as Mo surely would, that "The Child is father of the Man."

As I pondered these words, wondering what connections I might draw between this poem, Arthur's speech, Mo Hunt, and the many other great past and present English teachers at Deerfield, I did what they most probably would have done. I asked my students. Specifically, I asked them to tease out Wordsworth's paradox: How indeed might the child be father to the man when in plain fact he is not? Their responses were predictably varied and, I believe, go to the heart of English instruction at Deerfield today, and always. Let me share a few of them with you.

In response to my query, one sophomore wrote: ". . . youth and innocence govern us all." Another, a Floridian, replied: "At Deerfield, when I wake up in the morning and snow has painted everything white, I feel like there is nothing as perfect as that snowfall. And I don't even like snow! Children, who almost always love nature, show grownups how important nature is." One boy asserted: "We learn by experience! The child fathers the man by endowing him with experiences that last the rest of his life." "As people grow older they tend to forget the simple truths of childhood." And, finally: "Childlike enthusiasm and wonder is a great thing!"

Would you have said the same in 1967? I imagine that then, as today, your excursions to Rock or River were driven by a similar curiosity, innocence, and idealism, and that your willingness to explore afresh did not go unnoticed by your teachers. These are the very tenets in fact which spurred Mo Hunt to offer Art Clement a possibility that would carry both teacher and pupil well past the confines of a particular text, well beyond the world of dangling participles.

I'll let you in on a little secret: we do this job not so much because we love to teach, but because we love to learn. And that love, if we're unstinting in our sharing of it, becomes our students' love, your love. I'll bet everyone here a nickel that Mo Hunt introduced Art Clement to Ralph Ellison, not so that he could instruct Art all about African American writers. Rather, I wager, Mo did it to find out what he could learn about African American writers from Art. And if Art indeed "grasped his identity" as his teacher hoped he might, you can be sure that Mo's identity as a teacher was enhanced as well.

Mo Hunt offered Art Clement that book in 1966 for the same reason we all do, from Lambert to Littwin to Palmer; from Suitor to Scandling
to Stein. We do it because we love to learn, especially from those we teach.
Which reminds me of the time in 1969, my second year here, when I asked
the incomparable McGlynn whether he had yet read the latest novel by yet
another of the hot young writers he was always ferreting out on the margins.
"Read it?!" he exclaimed. "I haven't even taught it yet!" That, in a nutshell,
is what English at Deerfield continues to be about today. Curricular trends
come and go, bend this way and that as reeds in the wind. What remains
constant is curiosity, in 1967, in 1997. McGlynn's quip may speak volumes
about the 60s and 70s, but it also underscores the spirit of mutual inquiry
and discovery that binds us all yet.

Of course, the mantra of that time, your legacy to us, was "Question
Authority!" which we have been doing ever since, mindful that rooted in
"authority" is the word "author." Thanks to you, that straightforward menu
of classic authors you may recall dining from ad nauseum in the sixties
became, in the seventies, a banquet of electives ranging from "Literature of
the Seven Seas" to "Tales of the West," and, in 1977, one entitled
"Contemporary Song Lyrics," taught by a young Irishman named Peter
Fallon, now returned twenty years later as Deerfield's artist-in-residence and
Bicentennial poet! In 1987, the English Department offered twenty-four
spring term electives, including "Quest Narratives," "Afro-American
Literature," and "The Challenge of Spring." But as wide-ranging as this
menu had become by the mid-eighties, notably absent from the mix were
courses featuring women writers, a situation now addressed throughout the
English curriculum by a staff nearly equally comprised of women and men.

And if today we continue to follow your lead, questioning the
authority of all authors, the curiosity and commitment of our teachers
remain undiminished. While I hope you were both intrigued and pleasantly
surprised by the diversity of subject matter in this morning's classes, the
enthusiasm of your instructors should have been quite familiar to you.

If you remember sitting like ducks in a row, before a blackboard
which, if you studied with Bart Boyden, had your hopeless sentences
scrawled all over it, you might have been relieved this morning to sit, seminar style, around broad tables—the teacher not so much preceptor as fellow
quester, a benevolent guide through the dark wood of grammatical error. We
sit around tables nowadays the better to listen; answers aren't as easily come
by as they might have been in the early sixties, and we teachers need all the
help we can get. Indeed, the very notion of what constitutes a "classic" has

expanded over three decades to include important works from a variety of literatures, not all of them familiar to us, or even issuing from the English language. Today the Chinese boy across the table, the Bulgarian girl by his side, have much to teach us that transcends English. If your familiar classroom tools were pencils and chalk, you'll find pixels and mice the companions of Deerfield students today. But even as the medium has changed, the message remains the same: Tease order out of chaos. Worry words to life. Learn to love to learn.

In the 1960s you prepared assiduously for "floor talks" and vocabulary quizzes; today you'll find your young counterparts eagerly reciting declamations, and spinning CD-ROMS craftily supplied by the Princeton Review to prepare for SAT's. English instruction at Deerfield under Mr. Boyden was much like the school itself: orderly, rigorous, rooted in the "classics." Within that rigid context, however, there remained and remains an informing principle of mutual respect and youthful exuberance which guides us still, binding us each to each down through decades in our search for what is true and good in language and literature. In one very real sense, then, the child truly is the father of the man.

Let me close with one illustrative anecdote: In 1967, when many of you were here, I with my freshly minted master's degree drove to Deerfield on a snowy Saturday morning to be interviewed by Mr. Boyden, who asked me but a single question: "Do you like boys?" Before I could collect my wits to offer a reply—I had come prepared after all to discuss Milton, Shakespeare, gerunds! —he launched into the Tom Ashley story, and a half hour later I had a job. That was that. And while Mr. Boyden's query surely was that of a more innocent era, it still rings true for its implicit agreement with Wordsworth's tenet. Put simply, if you don't like kids, you're not likely to learn much from them, nor they from you. . . . (That Mr. Boyden announced his retirement shortly after this interview, I take to be entirely coincidental and not at all related to the appointment he had just made!) But, truth to tell, I do like boys, and girls, then and now, and so did Mo Hunt and so does every single one of my colleagues sitting among you today. And that at the last is what has bound this department for these three decades and many more. You saw it in the sixties; you saw it this morning.

Finally, in the spirit of the day, I'll conclude with an extra credit question: Which of the following names do you remember best? Choose from Column A: Shakespeare? Dickens? Twain? Ellison? or Column B: Lambert? McGlynn? Suitor? Hunt? A trick question, I trust you guessed, just as I trust that thirty years from now your sons and daughters, should we be lucky enough to have been taught by them, will sit in this Memorial Building remembering not so much the writers Bradstreet, Paley, Heaney or Walker, as the people: Driskill, Hannay, Henry, McNamara, Pandolfi, Thomas-Adams, and Wright. That's English at Deerfield, in 1967, in 1997. Thanks for coming today. It's been a pleasure learning with you.

*Tom Heise spoke on June 13, 1998, at the homecoming for the
Classes of 1990-1995, hosted by the History Department.
His talk was followed by a multimedia presentation by Grant Quasha '98.*

"AS NATURAL AS BREATHING": TEACHING HISTORY AT DEERFIELD

Thomas A. Heise

ABOUT A WEEK AGO I FOUND AN OLD BOOK in the English/History office. It is a college-level US History textbook that was probably in use in the 1930s here at Deerfield. Faulkner and Kepner's *America: Its History and People*, published originally in 1934 and revised in 1938, offers a vivid sense of history's evolution over the past sixty years. The narrative is short; its 700-page story of America stops in the 1920s. It is overwhelmingly political in its emphasis—there is scarcely any social history, there are no references to environmental issues, no pie charts graphing the number of hours of television Americans watch on average per day, and there is a certainty about its interpretation that is altogether at odds with our more equivocal age. Consider its summary of the Reconstruction period, for example.

Finding the Radical Plan a "miserable business" and a mean-spirited, vindictive invitation to corruption, Faulkner and Kepner salute the efforts of ex-Confederates "to bring back good sense and decency" to government. While the authors find little to like in the Ku Klux Klan, they fault the Klan's methods more than its ends; they praise the eventual "redemption" of the South by its white population as the welcome termination of a hideous experiment. They write:

> Upon a vanquished and prostrate foe and brother, the radical Republicans, bent upon revenge, forced a plan of reconstruction that placed the former slave above the master and left both to the mercy of unscrupulous carpetbaggers who plundered the states into bankruptcy. Reconstruction—a completely wrong term—had retarded the recovery of the South for a generation if not for a half-century.

Although the authors are slightly unsettled by the generations of suffering that redemption brought to the black population of the South, Faulkner and Kepner's greatest concern is for southern whites and national unity. It is on behalf of those interests that the authors lament that it took a full twelve years for the "disgraceful reconstruction episode [to be] closed." That the interests of the freedmen deserved at least equal consideration never seems to have occurred to them.

Contrast that interpretation of Reconstruction with the one put forth sixty years later in Paul Boyer's *Enduring Vision*, which several of us in the History Department now use. A synthesis of political, social, economic, diplomatic, and cultural history, Boyer's 1,100-page narrative raises to greater prominence historically neglected peoples and points of view. *Enduring Vision*, published in 1990 and revised for the second time in 1996, is available on CD-ROM and is now the most widely-adopted college-level US History text in America. On Reconstruction, Boyer writes:

> Looking back on the 1860s and 1870s, most late-nine-teenth-century Americans dismissed the congressional effort to reconstruct the South as a fiasco—a tragic interlude of "radical rule" or "black reconstruction," fashioned by carpetbaggers, scalawags, and Radical Republicans. With the hindsight of over a century, historians continue to regard Reconstruction as a failure, though of a different kind. No longer viewed as a misguided scheme that collapsed because of radical excess, Reconstruction is now widely seen as a democratic experiment that did not go far enough.

The error made by Radical Republicans, says Boyer, was not the attempt to build a biracial, democratic future in the South but instead their failure to use their legislative powers even more vigorously: first, by failing to insist on broad-based property redistribution so that the freedmen could be independent farmers and, second, by failing to protect blacks' civil rights indefinitely with military force. Today's historical consensus, one that is mindful of freedmen's interests, asserts that twelve years of Reconstruction was not tragically extended; it was tragically cut short.

What is the purpose of this comparison? In part, it is to demonstrate that the discipline of history is much more than a chronicle of the past. Historians define history as "the memory of things said and done," as "contemporary thought about the past," as a "mental construct." How we interpret the past, therefore, has much to do with the present; how we think about anything is a function not only of the knowledge we possess but also of our own life experiences and dispositions. While the stuff of history is "what happened," history's discipline and order come from how we learn to think about the past, an almost reflexive habit according to the eminent historian Gerda Lerner: "All human beings are practicing historians. . . . We live our lives; we tell our stories. It is as natural as breathing." That Paul Boyer would offer a different interpretation of Reconstruction than his predecessors makes perfect sense: Faulkner and Kepner grew to adulthood in the age of Jim Crow. Paul Boyer, on the other hand, entered the history profession during the civil rights movement.

In part, this comparison also suggests how history can be applied. We not only create history, we also use it. However inexact and interpretive, history holds out the hope of greater comprehension of the problems we encounter and a range of possible solutions. To cite but one example:

Many historians of the civil rights movement have been struck by President Kennedy's passivity on the question of racial justice, a posture at odds with the activism he seemed to promise as a candidate. John F. Kennedy, suggests the historian Harvard Sitkoff, "had been taught that radical Reconstruction was a mistake, that the solution to the race problem required moderation, not coercion." Perhaps Faulkner and Kepner's *America: Its History and People* was the textbook at Choate when young John Kennedy was a student there! The prevailing wisdom was that of social Darwinist William Graham Sumner, who asserted in 1907 that "stateways cannot change folkways." This idea is at the heart of Faulkner and Kepner's interpretation of Reconstruction, an interpretation that asserts the powerlessness of law to influence racial attitudes. This was the idea that prompted President Eisenhower to declare that "I don't believe that you can change the hearts of men with laws or decisions," an idea with which his Democratic successor Kennedy was in essential agreement and which helps explain Kennedy's inaction in matters related to civil rights. Martin Luther King, Jr., whose interpretation of American history was obviously very different, responded that "the law may not change the heart—but it can restrain the heartless." By the end of the 1960s, King's interpretation had prevailed, landmark legislation had been passed that ended statutory racism in America, and a new lesson of history had been written. Perhaps stateways can change folkways. Perhaps our teaching of history will influence our students and the decisions they make someday.

There are many reasons why we teach history at Deerfield. At the most pragmatic level, our students want to be prepared for Advanced

.Placement Exams and SAT IIs, and we are obliged to help them. There are more exalted reasons. We believe that the discipline of history is particularly well-suited for the development of a variety of skills: critical reading, analytical thinking, the detection of bias in primary and secondary works, the writing of interpretive, evidence-based essays, and historical research that draws upon a broad array of source material. It is partly to serve these ends that the Academy has as a diploma requirement the successful completion of a 10-20 page research paper.

The world that our students are growing into is multi-racial, multi-ethnic, multi-cultural, multinational, international and global in character. We seek therefore to acquaint them not only with a broadly inclusive American past, but also with the history of Europe, of Asia, of Latin America and of Africa. In Economics students begin to understand the nature of national and international markets and policy. But, aware of the rootlessness that can attend a globalized world, we have also developed a local history course to develop in our students a more rooted sense of place. The departmentally-developed *Deerfield Reader*, published in 1996 by American Heritage, is the principal text for that course.

Above all, we believe that the study of history enriches and improves us. According to historians, history "enlarges human experience" and "extends human life beyond its span." History enriches our lives by permitting us greater knowledge about where we came from and about what people before us thought and did. The study of history is, or at least ought to be, personally fulfilling and profoundly humanizing. History is an essential part of a liberal arts education. If education has been correctly defined as the transmission of a culture from one generation to the next, then the study of history has a central role to play in acquainting students with the world they will inherit. The study of history does not only seek preservation, however. It also seeks to equip students for the future. We study history to know and preserve what is good, to challenge and change what is not.

History is both ancient and surprisingly new. While we trace our discipline's lineage to Herodotus and Thucydides in the fifth century BC, the study of anything but classical history did not become standard fare in American secondary and higher education until the late nineteenth century. In 1880 there were only 11 history professors in the entire country. Since that time an entire profession has been created, a profession that has been contentious, quarrelsome, and disunified from the start. What do we argue about? We argue about the accuracy of interpretations—of Reconstruction, for example. We argue about the degree to which objectivity is attainable. We argue about whether a coherent narrative can be fashioned out of the outpouring of specialized, often-discordant knowledge from history's sub-fields. We argue about the purpose to which historical knowledge should be put.

While those are arguments we are aware of, the discussions we have had here at Deerfield tend to center on two other broad categories of questions: What should we teach? What do students need to know? Can we assure an extensive, sweeping knowledge of the past without making the passage through the centuries seem like a forced march? Can we assure student mastery of history without eliminating the delight that ought to accompany its study? What skills should our students possess? Can we compose a sense of the past that includes all of us and all parts of the world in meaningful ways? Can we "fit" as much history as we would like into one very short year?

How should we teach? Should we rely on lectures or discussion-based classes? To what degree should students direct their own learning? Should we teach history with a ten-pound textbook as a principal resource or rely on other means? What are the uses and limits of modern technology? Only one hundred years ago Americans heralded the installation of blackboards in every classroom as an educational breakthrough. Today President Clinton insists that every classroom in the country should be Internet-ready.

These questions defy easy or permanent answers. Our students are probably the best measure of our success in grappling with them. Grant Quasha, a cum laude graduate of the class of 1998, has returned today to share a project that he developed this year as a student in River, Valley, Rock, a senior-level, interdisciplinary course grounded in Deerfield, that integrates history, place-based literature, and environmental science. *Images of Deerfield*, a multimedia presentation prepared in consultation with Alan Fraker— Grant's teacher for two years in US History and River, Valley, Rock—suggests one way, among many, that students at Deerfield immerse themselves in the past and make history a part of themselves, a part of the world they will inhabit long after they leave here, and a part of the heritage they will leave to the generations that follow them.

This panel discussion took place on October 2, 1998
during the Grand Celebration weekend,
as part of "The Alumni Program for Our School."

A MOVING PICTURE:
VALUES AND TOLERANCE IN A CHANGING CULTURE

Robert B. Binswanger '48P, Steven D. Brill '68P, Elizabeth M. Clement S'66,
Eliot R. Cutler '64P, Ferrell P. McClean P'94, '98, Stephen G. Smith '67P

Stephen G. Smith '67P, Moderator. When Mimi Morsman and I were talking about this program, all the ideas were concrete, everyday, nothing too abstract. And then she got together with Eric and Meera and the Brain Trust up here and came back to me with the title: "A Moving Picture: Values and Tolerance in a Changing Culture." I felt as if I was back in an examination room at Deerfield with one of those blue books in front of me, and that cold sweat on my back, and a voice screaming inside my head saying, "Oh, my God. I didn't read this part!" In truth, I did read this part, and in fact everybody on this panel read this part. Deerfield is justifiably esteemed for the moral education it gives its students. When we were here, there were no written rules. You were simply supposed to know the difference between right and wrong, and when you had to think about it, you were better off assuming that what you were about to do was wrong. Traditional values, by which I loosely mean God, country, hard work, community standards, civic involvement, middle-class morality, are now tempered by the more modernist idea that people should be allowed to choose a style of life that's best for them and that others should tolerate that choice. I wonder if the panelists would offer thoughts on the changing balance between values and culture.

Steven D. Brill '68P. I think the major change is that there's much too much concentration today on what's legal, what is legally tolerable, what the law says one can do, as opposed to what is the right thing to do. Now the best example of that is, indeed, in the media. Basically, libel law allows Steve and any of his reporters, any of his editors, or me and any of my reporters, to do anything we want. And it doesn't make it right; it just makes it legally allowable. I'll just tell one story about that. A couple of years ago when I was running the Courtroom Television Network and we were sitting around trying to decide whether we should show pictures of O.J. Simpson's young kids, I said, "We're not going to do that. It invades their privacy." And someone said, "Well, everybody else is doing it." I said, "Well, we're not going to do it. I don't think we should do it." Then our newest employee, someone we had just hired from the Columbia Journalism School, said, "Well, of course we can do it. It's legal." And I said, "That's not the question."

I think in almost every area, too often the translation of what's right or wrong is whether the law says you can't do something. That's a result, in large part, of law being pervasive, indeed some would argue, intrusive, into so many areas of our lives. We are seeing a translation of the "right/wrong" debate into the "legal/illegal" debate. For example, I even heard that the Republicans wanted the FBI to investigate people who were spreading those rumors about Henry Hyde. Now the point is that it was wrong to spread those rumors. It was wrong, I think, to publish that stuff. But there was nothing illegal about it. It was just plain wrong.

Eliot R. Cutler '64P. A lot of my friends who became lawyers when I did have become depressed human beings. Many of them have left the law, including my wife. I think one of the reasons is that they have found themselves spending enormous amounts of time doing things that they never set out to do when they went to law school. They never set out to spend their time mastering arcane rules and regulations and helping people figure out how to get "just up to the line" of what the rules say you can do or can't do. They spend very little time dealing with questions of right and wrong and serious moral issues, which is what many of them went to law school to work on. When I was at Deerfield (as Steve Smith has said), there were no rules at all, and it was hard.

I remember then thinking, Deerfield has all this pressure for conformity, and this used to get under my skin. But I now think I understand that there was an unusually strong, almost gravitational, pull in this community toward the mean, toward a common set of norms and expectations of behaviors about what's right and what's wrong. Whoever you were at Deerfield, you came to expect that it was part of your job to make sure those values were respected. There is not much gravity right now in this country generally and certainly in Washington. We tolerate too much. We have elevated the notion of tolerance far above the core values themselves.

Ferrell P. McClean P'94, '98. As you can well imagine, in the high school class of 1964, there was not exactly an opportunity for me to be at Deerfield Academy. I happened to go to another school. Our motto was, "Be loyal to the royal in yourself," which basically said, if you were uncomfortable explaining what you were doing out loud, you probably shouldn't do it. I work for J.P. Morgan now. We use the same rule, in a way, when we're talking to people about how to use very precious, valuable inside information.

I'm going to take this also a different way. When I joined J.P. Morgan in 1969, there were no women bankers, somebody told me, because a woman couldn't possibly go to Chicago and stay in the Chicago Club and entertain there. That was the explanation I got. There were no ladies' rest rooms on the first two floors of the bank. There was a separate personnel department for women because there were only certain jobs that women could have. When I look at my whole working career, the change in values, the acceptance in corporate America of women in the work force, has been dramatically different. I am tremendously benefited by this, because I was at the front end of the wave; for example, when I walked into a meeting, I was usually the only woman, so people remembered who I was. The way values have evolved over the last 30 years has benefited corporate America as well as Deerfield.

Elizabeth M. Clement S'66. I need to say I'm not really nostalgic for a time when we had a singly defined, gravitational set of values to which all of us adhered as we were attempting, at least, to be the right kind of people. It would not have served me well. I can only speak for my experience as a Christian, as an African-American, as a woman at the close of the 20th century. Our newspapers have pushed us in the last few days to look at people who have made very important decisions for themselves and for others based on some notion of what was of value, and the range of difference in those decisions is extraordinary. Which makes me ask the question, who does help us to make our final decisions about values? Where is values work done?

A woman friend of mine not long ago asked the question, "Are the Ten Commandments still of value?" Let me just say that they are. They're here. They are present among us. I might say that they don't speak as often in our conversations as perhaps once they did. I might also say that they don't speak with the same value in our conversations as they once did. But I do think they speak, and the church must speak. The church must be in the business of helping persons who are busy making these decisions, to make them, and to make good ones.

Robert B. Binswanger '48P. Of course schools like ours teach values, including some that they probably don't intend to. One of the values in education that was practiced around the country was discrimination. We dis-

criminated against women. We discriminated in terms of race. It wasn't
called discrimination, but it was something that may or may not have been
taught in schools. The values that were taught in the 1700s were religious
values. People paid to go to school. The Bible was the text and the values of
the Bible were the only education available to the persons in school. After we
became a nation, particularly into the last century, the value that we wanted
to teach to the immigrant population was nationalism. We wanted them to
become patriotic and we worked hard at that. Even the elderly founding
fathers pushed that.

When we came to the beginning of this century, we had a different
immigrant population, and we wanted to educate them in terms of values.
They needed to become Americans and to speak English. We didn't value
their languages; we didn't value their cultures; we didn't value anything
about them, other than our concern that they learn American values: hard
work, obedience, sort of a "Simon Says" kind of education. We'll teach you,
you repeat, you learn it and then those will be the values that will help you
and the country.

To put this into perspective, I'll quote from McPhee and his book
about the Headmaster. There was a dean at Harvard whose name was Henry
Pennypacker, and he always used to say to Mr. Boyden, "After man is 30, he's
going to settle most of his social and moral problems in terms of his training in secondary school." Notice the word is training, not education. And
the response from Mr. Boyden in conversation with John McPhee was, "I
believe in a very normal life. It generally seeps in. I try to do the simple
things that a well organized home does." This says to me that the family is
very important in the teaching of values. And if a school like Deerfield is
family, and it is, it teaches the values of the society at a particular time.
That's all it can do.

Cutler. I think we're getting a bit confused about what core values are. I
think, for example, that tolerance is a core value. There have been periods in
our country's history and in this school's history when tolerance was not followed very closely in the behavior of the school or the community or the
nation. As a consequence, there was extraordinary bias towards people of
color, towards women, towards people with sexual preferences other than the
majority of people. And a lot of that intolerant behavior continues. I find it
extraordinary that we tolerate not telling the truth today, as I have found it
extraordinary that we have and continue to tolerate intolerance or bias.

Brill. I want to second something that Elizabeth said. I'm not sure those old values were really such great values, even at this place, in some respects especially at this place, way back when. More important than that, there seems to be a sense implicit in what Eliot said, that telling the truth is common and easy, but the way I would define a principle is that it is something hard to do. And sometimes telling the truth, which is of course a core principle, is hard to do, and very often people are unable to do it. I don't think that is something unique to 1998 or to 1968, when I graduated from this place. People do lie all the time about things that are hard to tell the truth about. That doesn't make them good people or bad people, but I really don't think we should sit under this tent, under the illusion that we've really slipped back from the good old days. I'm sure that in the good old days when I was here, someone told me that it was really good and appropriate for me as a Jewish person to go to church on Sunday at 10:00. And I don't think it was true.

Smith. Clearly, telling the truth is a paramount value at this school. Just as clearly, in a disciplinary proceeding, it may be more important than the infraction under consideration in the first place. I wonder whether that same premium on telling the truth is something shared by the country at large or are we sitting in Happy Valley here, telling the truth to each other.

Clement. It's the atmosphere of trust that is the value to be protected. Trust is always, always risky. It requires acceptance of the risk, but trust also requires grace, and if you'll permit me to say it, forgiveness. The models on this campus, in this institution over its 200 years, are certainly there. There are few of us who have not lied. The consequences we face are in the deterioration of the atmosphere of trust, which is the soup that permits us to live together in some sort of way that lets each of us be who we are.

One of the things that's been most extraordinary for me in the last few weeks has been watching the cosmic lack of grace. Elected officials and other prominent personalities have been simply unwilling to offer grace to anyone. I raise the question in the context of something I think everyone in this room has at least heard of. It's "The Golden Rule"; you do unto others as you would have them do unto you. There was a time when that had a certain value, but my youngest son, who is now 14, when he was seven told me it was the most ridiculous thing he'd ever heard. I suspect that he's carrying the day now, because it is a terribly difficult principle which few of us are capable of living, even when it's very important that we do so.

McClean. I had an interesting conversation with my 18-year-old Deerfield daughter. We were talking about the current situation in Washington and she was saying, "Mom, the president's business is his own business. It's personal, we don't need to worry about it." And I said, "He lied to me. He lied to everybody. How do I know now when he's telling the truth? How can I trust him any more?" But what rang true for the two of us in that conversation was that she tends to trust people, as I do, and basically believes that people are telling the truth.

Binswanger. I find it interesting in our society that we have no term that we use called "black lies." We do use a term called "white lies." The worry I have in our society is that we all lie. We all lie when we say, "I'm too busy. Don't tell them I'm home," when the phone rings. We lie at the table when we're discussing things and young children listen in on the conversation. We lie in our business affairs. We lie in our interactions with our spouses, our mates. It's a common thing, and the problem of lying in Washington is put in the perspective of how we view lying. As one of the other panelists said, lying is just plain wrong.

Brill. It is easy to draw big black lines and make bold statements, you know, "Lying is wrong." People do lie. That doesn't make it right. But to acknowledge reality is to say there are certain kinds of lies that go to the core of who we are and what we are and how we can exist together. Certainly, lying in something involving the disciplinary process is very important. Certainly, lying in a legal proceeding ought to be considered to be extremely important. I just resist the notion that Americans are more tolerant today and just don't like the generalization that today is better or worse than it used to be when it comes to lies or anything else.

For example, in one of our kids' schools, a staff member was fired. Everybody knew it. I mean eight-year-olds knew it; nine-year-olds knew it. And the letter comes from the headmaster saying this person has decided to resign after only eight months on the job, to seek other opportunities. That is a very destructive kind of lie, sending a message to kids. On the other hand, why embarrass and humiliate that person by sending out a memo that says, "We've fired him because he's a hopeless incompetent." So, sometimes you make those compromises, and I think we need a lot more subtlety and a lot more sophistication for that argument.

Smith. Telling the truth can have, in that context, an ironic effect. Some years ago I had the unpleasant experience of being fired. The usual corporate statement went out saying that I was going to be pursuing other business opportunities, none of which I had a clue about. The *Times* and the *Washington Post* called and they said, "Gee, I hear you're going to pursue other business opportunities." And knowing that Page Six would be back the next day saying I'd been fired, I thought, well, my family's been through it once, why go through it twice. So I said, "No, I was fired." And the *Times* reporter said, "What?!" It turned out, after I'd said I was fired to about four reporters, the people who fired me called and said, "Could we sue for peace? Could we stop this? This is really embarrassing for us." So it's a great lesson.

Cutler. In my experience, at least, in politics, in practicing law for 30 years, I must say I believe that there is an expanding sphere of what's OK. What bothers me most about our current dilemma is that it seems to be pushing a lot of people further in that direction. I think that's extremely troubling, because it's very hard to do politics in this country, it's very hard to do business in this country, it's very hard to practice law in this country, if you can't have any confidence that the person with whom you're dealing is telling the truth.

Clement. I don't know this, but I have a sense that once upon a time, we operated, not just at Deerfield, but in this country, on some general set of values that most of us understood. "Lying is wrong" was in there. At the close of the twentieth century, many of the values that were included in the general understanding of what was right and wrong are still there, but others are not. We believe these truths to be self-evident, that all men, and perhaps women, are endowed by their creator with certain inalienable rights. It is the premise upon which this country was based, but for almost 200 years, we lived as though it were not there. And we did that in good faith; we did that respecting one another; we set up institutions that preserved the difference between that underlying value and the things we were actually doing. It strikes me that if lies are the problem, so is hypocrisy. Yet Thomas Jefferson was on to something, an ideal which we continue to hope to live.

Kerry Emanuel said something instructive this morning. In science, they are seeing now that the reductionist kind of approach to scientific problems simply doesn't work any more. I want to submit to you, that reductionist, even nostalgic, approaches to the complex issues in our society today cannot be answered with Band-Aids or bumper stickers either. The challenge that the scientific world is facing is the challenge all of us are facing, to find new and appropriate ways, ways that have a certain integrity that will permit us to deal with the differences and the shifts among us.

Smith. One of the interesting aspects of the greater weight given to tolerance today is that thinkers from G.K. Chesterton to William Bennett have worried that tolerance taken too far can lead to indifference, even moral exhaustion. Should we be more judgmental? Should we be less tolerant?

Cutler. I fear, as I said a few moments ago, a sphere of behavior growing so large that we lose some bedrock core values. It would have been very difficult to have made the kinds of progress we've made in repairing the things that have been wrong with this country for so long, if there hadn't been enough people who were willing to tell the truth.

McClean. There's another side of me that says, what does being judgmental do if it doesn't change anything? You remember my little anecdote about the Chicago Club. When finally Morgan agreed I could be a banker after I'd been there for about 10 years, they said, "Let's go out and entertain some clients. And let's go play golf." That sounded great to me. They said, "Why don't you be in charge of the outing; let's go to National Golf Links on Long Island." I said, "That's great, except National doesn't let women eat lunch there; I'm not going to entertain my clients. Let's go to another club." So I held the outing there, but to my great surprise they'd planned the lunch in the men's bar. I had half a dozen clients there, but I ate in the dining room while they ate in the men's bar. What's happened since then is that corporate America will not have outings at country clubs that discriminate, and that the country clubs need the revenue, so they've changed. Sounds like a little thing, but basically, when corporations have withdrawn their support, institutions have changed.

Brill. If you think about standards and discipline as opposed to being judgmental, you come out in a different place. For example, I once had an English teacher here, who's sitting over there. (Now this isn't anything that rises to the level of judgmental, or even rises to the level of being a principle, although for me it became one.) Mr. Lambert used to razor blade out the word "very," if you put it in an essay. I remember this because my writing would have all these holes in it. Now I always thought that was a cool thing to have that kind of stubborn standard about something and stick to it. Indeed to this day, I defy any of you to find the word "very" in any publication that I'm responsible for, because I have copied him, although I don't use the razor blade.

Now that's a small thing, but we can take stands about certain things. I have a rule, for example, that if we ever find a reporter who cheats even by a dollar on an expense account, where we can really figure out that it's deception, we fire the reporter immediately, and we tell them this in advance. The reason is that we send them out to interview people and to accurately write what people are telling them, and we trust them. If you can't trust the person for a dollar, why would you trust them with the pages of your publication. I don't think that person's a horrible person who shouldn't get a job somewhere else, who can't be redeemed. I'm not sitting in judgment. But we have a standard and we have to keep to it.

Clement. Persons like Mr. Lambert who have powerful commitments and standards are extremely important to all of us. In fact, most religious traditions have such very clear standards. If I had a lament, it would be that somehow the voice of the church has stopped being in this conversation, and it has stopped being in conversation with a great many young people.

Cutler (responding to a student question). I don't think there can be anyone in this tent, even our headmaster, who I think is as close as you can get; there can't be anyone in this tent who is perfect. I noticed actually, you were wearing clothes. And somebody suffered, or worked hard or got exploited for the clothes you're wearing. That does not make you a bad person, I assure you of that. There is a huge difference, I think, between knowing in the abstract that as we went to sleep last night there are people starving, and not getting out of bed immediately to do something with our money and our resources to help; there is a difference between that and riding down the street, seeing someone who needs an ambulance, and just riding past that person. There are no absolutes in the world. One of the great things about an education here is that you get the perspective of seeing that the world is not black and white, because most of the time when you see the world only in blacks and whites you tend to see only the black.

McClean (in response to a question about women in the work force). In the investment banking area where I focus, there are a lot of concerns of young women coming into the business, because of the lifestyle, because it's very demanding. I tend to believe that in most of the places where I have been and where I see women working, it has been somewhat harder for women than it has been for men. I'm sure that that's also true for people of color. But they are now basically meritocracies and if you perform well you will be rewarded.

Clement. I agree with everything that Ferrell has said, but I want to go just to the next step. If the meritocracy is something you think ought to change, it will be yours to make into a new model. I believe that things are better, and I think some of that has to do with the fact that women and African-Americans and Asians are players, and that we have become more diverse in terms of the gifts that we are able to offer. Let me put it this way; the church hasn't got a terribly good record on this. They're not always nice to women, especially women who dare to want to be in ordained ministry. But as we bring those changes to the model, the model itself is changing.

Binswanger (in response to an audience comment that we live in a "blame culture"). You are saying that you'd like to focus our attention on the fact that [Clinton] has also blamed his behavior. He sought to avoid personal responsibility for his behavior and blamed what he did on others' actions, on circumstances, and that it's not just Bill Clinton who has done this, but that it is a problem for all of us and a growing problem of society. I happen to think you're absolutely right. I couldn't have said it any better than you did and I'm not going to try.

I'd like to make a comment to the students, so I'd like the rest of you not to listen. You live in a society that is still very young. We're an unfinished nation, an imperfect union, trying to do better. The society you live in is deep in cynicism, and if you went to the panel this morning, you must wonder, because we don't have answers, what is in there for you. There's plenty for you. All you have to do is act. You don't need us to give you the moral direction. There are plenty of things that need to be done in this society. Don't do them all. Just choose one and do it, because we all need your help.

Bend of the River

Photograph - Frances and Mary Allen, c.1909
Memorial Hall Museum
Pocumtuck Valley Memorial Association
Deerfield, Massachusetts

IV. The Contributing Life.

A refrain of gratitude and praise for Deerfield's work in community service sounded in countless speeches and conversations through the Bicentennial observances. While admiring the extensive programs in place, speakers nonetheless urged their listeners to do more, and to make such service a lifetime habit. We took our title for this section from Senator Chafee's point that the value of a school may be measured by the number of its graduates who devote their lives to the welfare of others.

*Senator Chafee delivered this address
at the Bicentennial Convocation, September 12, 1997.*

"NEVER GIVE IN"

John H. Chafee '40P

IN THE MIDST OF WORLD WAR II, WINSTON CHURCHILL, then leading his nation through the most perilous period in its long history, returned to his old school, Harrow, to address the students. It was with understandable anticipation that the school gathered to hear its most famous graduate and a man recognized as the greatest orator in the English-speaking world. Following his introduction, Churchill strode to the front of the stage, thrust his bulldog-like chin forward, glowered at his audience and in thunderous tones said, "Never give in. Never give in. Never, never, never, never—in nothing great or small, large or petty—never give in except to convictions of honor and good sense." He paused and returned to his seat. The students were left a bit bewildered. Was there more to come? No. That was it, all 22 seconds of it. But there wasn't a person present that evening that did not clearly remember that speech and its message. And it certainly set a record for brevity!

Short though it was, Churchill's admonition reflected a characteristic that was deeply woven into the philosophy of those who founded Deerfield Academy and of those who nurtured it into greatness. It was only because those leaders would never give in that this school has lasted 200 years.

Two hundred years is a long time in our young Republic. John Adams was sworn in as our second president the year Deerfield Academy opened its doors. Andover and Exeter had been founded several years previously, but those are the only major schools older than Deerfield. There has been an abundance of adversity for Deerfield Academy over these 200 years. For its first 105 years it was a town academy of modest achievements—able to give a fair education to the children of the farmers and others in the valley. Those children in the area with ambitions to go to college, such as Helen Childs, later to become Mrs. Boyden, attended Greenfield High School, which offered a better education.

By the early 1900s, it was questionable whether the Academy could, or should, survive. The story of Mr. Boyden, just graduated from Amherst, arriving in August 1902 to be Headmaster, is now legend. There were only 14 pupils enrolled, two in the senior class, and an aura of discouragement permeated the school.

Few people better represented the aforementioned Churchillian philosophy of never giving in than Mr. Boyden. He tirelessly sought to recruit more students. Gradually he increased the enrollment. With the encouragement of Tom Ashley, class of 1911, who returned as a teacher, Deerfield opened a boarding department, drawing students from across New England and some from further away. It is so fitting that every year the seniors are told the remarkable story of Tom Ashley. He had such a key role in planning the future of this school and in encouraging Mr. Boyden. As have scores of Deerfield graduates, I have visited the beautiful Aisne-Marne American Military Cemetery near Chateau-Thierry, France, and have gone to Plot A, Row 6, Grave 63, where lies young Marine 2nd Lieutenant Thomas W. Ashley. He was killed attacking a German machine gun nest in nearby Belleau Wood in June 1918.

The loss of Tom Ashley was a terrible blow to Mr. Boyden. The two shared similar aspirations for this school, with Ashley frequently being the bolder. But Mr. Boyden persevered. He didn't give in. Post World War I years found Deerfield Academy growing, with new dormitories and classroom buildings. One hundred fifty pupils were enrolled. But the school was fiscally very frail. Crucial to its financial well-being was the $20,000 per year the Town of Deerfield contributed to the school for educating some of the town's children. It seemed like a death knell for the Academy when a new law in 1924 declared no public funds could be used to subsidize partially private schools, which Deerfield was. The town contribution must end.

That "never give in" spirit was still part of Deerfield and of its friends. The school was rescued by the extraordinarily generous action of the headmasters of Andover, Exeter and Taft, who solicited supporters of their own schools to contribute adequate funds to save Deerfield. What wonderful men they were, and what a tribute to Mr. Boyden and the work he'd done at this school.

By the decade of the 30s it was clear that Deerfield was one of the great schools of the country. Mr. Boyden had led it to greatness in the short period of 30 years. It clearly was different from the other great schools. There were no printed rules—everyone was expected to behave himself, and if he didn't, Mr. Boyden stopped him somewhere in the course of the day and expressed keen disappointment at such behavior. He referred to it as "high school stuff."

Athletics were supreme, with a team for everyone. How nice it is that this is still true. I noted with pleasure in this fall's athletic schedule Deerfield has eight different soccer teams with scheduled opponents. There was no true library, just a small room in the basement with limited hours; but money was found to build five beautiful squash courts. There was a music room—the small room to the left as you enter the gym. It seemed to be constantly locked, and I never set foot inside it. Music appreciation consisted of a splendid marching band, an annual Gilbert and Sullivan production and vigorous singing, especially at the Sunday night sings. Most of the hymns I know were learned at those sings.

If there were art classes, they were unknown to most of the students. The courses were rigorous and extremely well taught by teachers such as Russ Miller, Dick Hatch, Bartlett Boyden, and of course Mrs. Boyden and many others who made the work interesting. There was plenty of memory work and rightfully so. Those vocabulary tests of Bartlett Boyden's taught us humility and attentiveness. How could we not know the meaning of so many words in *Silas Marner*? Russ Miller showed us how to outline, and that has served me well ever since. And the dates he drilled into us provide benchmarks to our knowledge of history. Knowing that Louis XIV reigned from 1643 to 1715 has proven far more useful than you might think.

About this time in the 30s there appeared an unusual article in *Fortune Magazine* entitled, "Twelve of the Best American Schools." The schools the authors chose consisted of many that you or I might list today. Let me give you that list of 60 years ago, in order of the schools' founding: Andover, Exeter, Deerfield, Lawrenceville, The Hill, St. Paul's, St. Mark's, Groton, Thacher, Kent, Hotchkiss, and Avon Old Farms. Cited as close alsorans were Choate, Taft, Milton, Middlesex, St. George's, and Loomis. Curiously of the first 12, all but three are in New England, and of the next six, all are in New England. At that time when the article appeared, Exeter's endowment led the way with eight million dollars, with Deerfield in the bottom tier with $330,000. Tuition at each of the schools was about $1,500, with Andover and Exeter at slightly less. The article was not highly flattering to these schools. Said the authors, "By and large, and with only qualified exceptions, it must be said that the expensive private schools of America have done next to nothing to justify their existence."

The thesis of the authors is that the graduates of such schools must perform a special service to society; that those schools should teach a social conscience and a political sense. Research of the authors indicated that, as of that date 60 years ago, from the ranks of the 67,000 graduates of the 12 schools had come only 27 U.S. Senators, one member of the Supreme Court, and one President of the U.S.—Franklin D. Roosevelt of Groton. Since the article appeared, there has been one additional President of the U.S. from the 12 schools mentioned in the article: George Bush from Andover. There are currently six members of the Senate who have graduated from those schools: three from Exeter, two from Deerfield and one from St. Paul's.

Why should we even spend time considering criticism leveled 60 years ago (criticism that I believe is flawed in many respects)? What determines the value of a school is not solely how many graduates go into full-time government service, but how many live contributing lives—in, for example, education, where Deerfield graduates have been especially strong, or in the professions such as law or medicine, where we have just heard from several distinguished Deerfield graduates; in the ministry or arts; in banking, business or manufacturing, where jobs are created and the international competitive position of our country is determined.

While the criticisms referred to can to some degree be dismissed, it is worth reminding ourselves that government at every level—town and city, county, state and national—needs every bit of able talent it can recruit. While as a nation we seem to extol "less government" and cry, "Get government off our backs," we at the same time recognize the need for government to protect or improve life for ourselves and for our children. Thirty-five years ago there was no EPA, no Clean Water or Clean Air Acts, no Endangered Species Act, and there was no Medicare. No one dreamed that one's outboard motorboat would have to be registered

I'm fresh from our summer home in Maine where no longer does one heave one's trash into an abandoned gravel pit labeled "The Town Dump." Instead one follows—or tries to follow—elaborate directions pertaining to garbage, as opposed to returnables, as contrasted with recyclables. Each of these categories is disposed of at a separate location, miles apart from one another. These major or minor laws did not come about because of ultra-zealous government bureaucrats wanting to garner more power over citizens' lives. These laws were enacted, frequently reluctantly, in response to genuine concerns of our citizens.

For example, what will be the aftermath of the loss of 11 people, nearly all European tourists, drowned last month by a flash flood in Northern Arizona while on a guided tour where the guides are subject to no regulatory oversight? Probably by this time next year, Arizona will have some regulations on the books pertaining to the training of such guides. More government. Government is here to stay, struggle though we may to restrain its growth. What's all this got to do with Deerfield?

This Republic of ours needs good people, the best we can find to run our government on all levels, whether it's serving on the town library board or trying to devise a method of compassionately reducing our welfare rolls or trying to reach international trade accords. We need more than good administrators who will run a tidy ship and make sure the books balance. We hope that this school will continue to provide a superior education to you, its students, inculcating in you a sense of service to our society; that your minds will be stretched, your imaginations stirred and that you will learn to think, not just of the next year, but also of the next five decades. We seek broad-gauge minds—call it a vision for the future.

Hopefully the young men and women at this school will be imbued with that tenacity which is such a part of this institution's history. And this point I particularly wish to stress: at Deerfield may the students' sense of courage be strengthened. Our nation needs citizens with the courage to swim against the tide when so required; to do the right—but perhaps not the popular—thing.

It is my experience in Congress that most of the members know what has to be done to solve our nation's most pressing problems, such as how to save Social Security or Medicare for future generations. It is not ignorance that prevents solutions; it is lack of courage—a fear that the voters might not like the necessary stiff medicine. We want Deerfield to have exciting teachers, a broadly diverse student body with an abundance of scholarship students, and students from foreign nations. We hope it will take a chance on some students that haven't shown great potential. Would seemingly morose, certainly uncommunicative 14-year-old Tom Ashley be admitted to Deerfield today? I hope so.

While there is an air of permanence about this great Academy, its continued existence is not preordained. It grew to greatness in just 30 years and presumably could decline as fast. We have seen scores of companies or institutions, which once seemed so strong, close or be merged out of existence: Pan American Airways, the Pennsylvania Railroad, Woolworth's, Montgomery Ward—where are they now? Some are gone, the rest fallen from greatness.

Each of us, in our home states, has seen venerable hospitals, fraternal orders, social clubs, schools or even colleges struggle, barely survive or disappear. Deerfield will celebrate future anniversaries only if it does its job of providing a superior education for its students, and if those of us who care about this school support it with our time, talent, and treasure.

Let us meet that challenge! Let us be worthy of our heritage.

*Elizabeth Clement offered this sermon at the Grand Celebration Worship Service
at the First Church of Deerfield, on Sunday, October 4, 1998.*

THE GIFTS OF MEMORY

The Reverend Elizabeth Mitchell Clement S'66

2 TIMOTHY 1:1-6, LAMENTATIONS 3:19-24, PSALM 137:1-6

GRACE, MERCY AND PEACE BE UNTO YOU, members of the Deerfield family,
celebrants of this Bicentennial, beloved of God.

It is somehow fitting that we have as our New Testament reading
for today the correspondence between a master teacher and his best student.
Paul is writing from prison to Timothy who is serving a church and, not surprisingly, is having some difficulty there. Timothy is quite young, and he
comes from a mixed heritage—his mother is a Jew and his father a Greek—
and, besides, he has been called to lead the faithful into a New Age. Any one
of these factors might make for trouble in most churches I know.

Paul's letter to Timothy begins, then, with an invitation to remember, to look back. He recalls Timothy to the places and the people who
shaped him—that is, his mother and grandmother, their faith community,
and Paul himself, his mentor.

If Paul had been free to travel, his concern for his young friend
might have occasioned a visit. Had they actually been together in this
remembering, I imagine they would have told stories: stories of their days on
the road together, birthing new churches across the Diaspora, preaching and
teaching together. I imagine they would have laughed as they looked back
on some of their near-misses, as they marveled at some of the things they got
away with. They might have grown quiet, even tearful, as they remembered
friends and colleagues who were no longer in this world. They might have
sung songs from those earlier times and been surprised at the flood of emo-
tions that washed over them.

If this had not been a letter, it might well have been an invitation to
Timothy to come back for a reunion, a weekend together not perhaps unlike

the one we have shared here at Deerfield. But Paul cannot go to Timothy and so he sends this letter, this pastoral letter, and in doing so he means to build up and reassure, to comfort and even to embolden young Tim. In fact, his letter means to bear Paul's very presence to that distant place, to lay hands on the boy, to put an arm around his shoulder.

If you are a young person like Timothy, you might wonder what the point is of reminiscing. What's the point of reliving the past? It is a good question. There is an interesting paradox at work here. Paul is calling the past into present memory so as to free Timothy for the demands of the future. We don't know exactly what problems Timothy was facing; we only know that he was struggling and, from his own jail cell, Paul—forever the teacher—wanted to get words of encouragement to him. Is this not the sort of letter Mr. Boyden might have written to Tom Ashley, or Mr. Widmer to any of you?

Paul knows his student very well, he knows his gifts, and he knows the perils of his work. But, just as Paul will not be held captive by his present predicament, he seeks a way in turn to get Timothy beyond his own present predicament. He has a two-point strategy: he will pray night and day —do you know how often your teachers pray for you?— and he will invite Timothy to remembrance. Mind you, Paul is interested in getting Timothy beyond the narrow story of his current circumstances, not because he does not take the present seriously, or because he would spare the young man the difficult business of growing up. No, Paul's strategy intends to equip Timothy with a broad enough perspective to make sense of this very experience.

To use the images of the Bicentennial Poet, Peter Fallon, Paul wants Timothy to see "the plain where the human heart's potential hovered" and also to see "Again the sun rises on Pocumtuck Mountain Range as it has done so often, so many times." Paul calls Timothy back to the emotional and spiritual geography in which the young man was shaped, where he was formed, the experiential landscape in which he began to know himself, and to know God's love, and to recognize his own vocation, the meaning for his life. His purpose in remembering Timothy is to re-gather Timothy, to re-focus him, to re-collect him, and to re-center him in the authentic identity he had before he came to these troubles. The purpose of their "reunion" is to strengthen Timothy for what he has yet to do. A reunion, Eric Widmer said yesterday, points to the days of glory yet to come.

In our other texts for today from Psalms and Lamentations, we see the same strategy employed, using the past in service of the future. The psalmist, writing from the Babylonian captivity, where the future is most uncertain, cries out, [author's paraphrase] "If I forget you, O Jerusalem, my hand will wither, my tongue will stick." Yes, we wept when we remembered Zion, but thank God for Zion, where I became myself, who I really am, not who my persecutors would have me think am.

The writer of Lamentations says much the same: [author's paraphrase] "I look at the craziness of the world around me and I start to feel I have no home, no place to be, and my soul sinks within me." Here, suddenly, the mood changes: "But this I call to mind, and therefore have hope: the steadfast love of God never ceases; God's mercies never come to an end. They are new every morning!" The gift of God's steadfast love is my portion; the writer fairly shouts, "I will hope in God!" Paul says to Timothy, "I remind you to rekindle the gift—stir it up!—the gift of God that is in you." In that you will find hope.

The memory of God's love for Timothy, the memory of his mother's love, his grandmother's love, his teacher's love, can renew and refresh, sustain and empower Timothy for the work he has before him. These memories are timeless gifts; they are both old and new every morning. It is the gift of God's love the teacher recalls to his student so as to frame the claims of the present moment, and to free him for the demands of the next. Mr. Boyden might have said, "Timothy, look to the hills, boy. Look to the hills."

The memory of God's steadfast love goes behind us and before us. Like the hills surrounding this valley, the memory of God's grace and mercy both cradles us and stirs us to flight. The gifts of that memory are too many to name but, since I've come a long way, may I suggest a few:

The gift of memory is imagination, perhaps even prophesy. The gift of memory—of a history shared with God—is an authentic, personal vision. The gift of memory—of roots—is wings. The gift of memory—of boundaries—is freedom. The gift of memory—of a well-reflected past—is a bold future. "Rekindle the gift that is within you." Stir up the gift of God that is in you, the steadfast love of God that is in you, entrusted to you according to God's own purpose and grace. Look to the hills, friends, and remember God's great and steadfast love. That is the gift that is in you. Stir it up!

Amen.

This contribution is drawn from a transcription of the video tape of
President Bush's speech at the Commencement exercises for the Class of 1997.
He spoke informally, without a prepared text.
The "Alexander" he refers to is his great-nephew, Alexander Ellis IV '97,
and "Robert" is the student Commencement speaker, Robert B. Dunphy '97.

SOME ADVICE FROM AN OPTIMIST

George H. W. Bush, Former President of the United States

I'M VERY PLEASED TO BE HERE AT THIS SPARTANLY NON-POLITICAL EVENT. But I would be remiss if I didn't single out two parents, not for partisan political reasons. The Governor of the State of New Jersey and the Governor of the State of New York are with us, and that says something wonderful about a Deerfield graduation. I salute both of them. I hope I haven't disappointed any of you by not entering this field by parachute. Seriously, it was suggested. A lot of people asked about the jump I had made recently, whether it was frightening. I said the only frightening part was telling Barbara. And she said, "I haven't seen a free fall like that since the election of 1992."

I want to congratulate, certainly, the Class of '97 and the distinguished faculty that this institution is known for—the spirit of the place—and all those proud parents of the graduating class. I want to make just two points today. The first is that, when I look at the world today, I'm an optimist. Maybe that's because at almost 73 years of age, I've seen how far we've come. I know that a lot of people, especially young people, are concerned about the future, and we've seen a lot of changes taking place in the world over the past few years. Change always breeds uncertainty. But consider this. Way back when I was where you are today, in June of 1942, about to graduate, fascism and imperialism threatened the world. Across the country millions of kids, sitting where you are sitting, graduating, were joining the service right away to fight in World War II. Fifty-five years ago, I waited one day after the Andover graduation. When I became 18 on June 12, I went in and did what most other American kids were doing, signed up to fight against fascism and imperialism.

Then, beginning in the 1950s, following that "war to end all wars," we saw the Cold War, a conflict which divided our world with ideological boundaries, divided it into two armed camps, two super-powers, enemies with nuclear arsenals targeted at each other. The whole world had to choose sides. At the depth of this conflict, our world stood on the brink of Armageddon, and throughout this era, it remained marked by hostility and distrust. Your parents, many of them, were taught to hide under their desks to avoid nuclear fall-out, the catastrophe that might come about because one of the two super-powers fired that fatal shot. And then not too long ago, during the time I was privileged to serve as president, the conflict and suspicions of the past suddenly and dramatically gave way to a new era of hope and cooperation and peace. Just as important, the barriers dividing our world were breached, not by the forces of war, but by the force of ideas. Shots weren't fired when that Berlin Wall finally fell. Shots weren't fired when the unthinkable happened, when Germany was unified. Nor when Eastern Europe and the Baltic States were set free. Nor when the Soviet Union, as we knew it, simply imploded.

The people wanted freedom. All the barbed wire and the concrete in the world couldn't stop them, and today the world continues to turn toward freedom and democracy. Again, I know that many young people don't feel as optimistic as I do. And it's not just here in this country. A couple of years ago I was in Eastern Europe, and I saw on television a young Hungarian girl about the age of the graduating seniors here today. She looked beautiful, and she was beautifully dressed and coiffed. She was saying, though, "My generation doesn't have any hope. We're discouraged. The economy's bad in Hungary." I'm thinking to myself, "Have you looked over your shoulder into recent history? Do you remember when, maybe, your uncle was being crushed by Soviet tanks rolling through the streets of your capital? Don't you remember what it was like when you didn't have the freedom to speak on television as you now are, even though you are complaining all the way?" They felt they had no chance and things were bad. I was shocked at what she said.

I think that we have to put things in proper perspective. Indeed, for decades our nation struggled waging the Cold War, but today we see how the sacrifices of the American people, the policies of many of my predecessors and the vigilance of those who served in uniform, have paid off. Simply put, as we stand here today, our future, your future, is far safer, the prospects for peace far brighter than ever before. Reverend McKelvey, in the Invocation, called it "a vibrant future," and that is exactly what I think you are walking into.

As we near the end of this century, I'm reminded of words by one of my predecessors, Teddy Roosevelt. He said, "Much has been given to us and much is rightly expected of us. And we have duties to others and duties to ourselves, and we can shirk neither." I hope you will all find some time down the road to learn something about public service, indeed about politics, and eventually, to find a way to get involved in what Teddy Roosevelt appropriately call "the arena." Regrettably it's kind of ugly today: charge and counter-charge, unaccountable adversarial journalism.

I still believe, as I expect the two governors here today do, that politics is a noble calling. Certainly public service is. With this sentiment in mind we've started, down in Texas, the George Bush School of Government and Public Service at Texas A&M. If we can inculcate this concept of service into just a handful of young men and women, we will have done something wonderful. One person getting involved can make a difference. More importantly, I hope we can help the future leaders of this country understand that character does matter. I love those awards passed out here today; character matters. The values that you've learned here at Deerfield matter. Robert touched on it in a light, humorous way, but I expect he learned from every little encounter with those characters you have drifting around this marvelous campus.

Of course we all have our own definitions of success. Each of you has your own. Let me give you mine, which is my second main point today. I believe that any definition of a successful life must include service to others. It is just that simple. When I was privileged to serve as president, I often defined that concept as being one of a thousand points of light. That means individuals getting involved in their communities and helping make lives better, helping make places to live better. Last month Barbara and I were pleased to go to the Philadelphia Summit, where for three days we met with volunteers from all over the country. That summit was so beautifully run by Colin Powell, who is continuing with his passionate interest in service to others. I know that some people looked at what happened at the Philadelphia Summit as all show biz and glitz, and there was some of that. Who wouldn't like to stand up there, as I had to do, with Brooke Shields, to pass out an award? The teleprompter went off, broke right there on the spot, so we just stood there, kind of hugging. It was a marvelous feeling; somebody had to do it. And then of course, Barbara did the same thing with John Travolta. It was a tough duty. But the spirit of Philadelphia is already happening right here in your communities. If you go to Greenfield, Turners Falls, you'll find volunteers solving problems locally that are plaguing our country nationally. You should be a part of that now and wherever you go in the years ahead.

The point is that you don't have to be a president to be a leader, and you don't have to be a first lady to touch the life of someone else. All you

have to do is care and get off the sidelines and do something about teen preg-
nancy or disadvantaged kids who need tutoring or just being a mentor to a
kid who has lost his way. If I could leave you with one message, it's that one
person can make a difference, and that every one of us here has the power to
lift lives. Everyone can serve. Remember when Barbara went up to speak at
Wellesley? Those girls were going to get her. They had their signs ready. She
was the wife of someone; she wasn't a professional woman. And she disarmed
them. She took Raisa Gorbachev with her, a real communist. And the girls
didn't know whether to put their signs down or hold them up, so they took
the signs down. They didn't want to hurt Raisa's feelings. When the signs
were down, Barbara said this to them, and that wonderful audience warmly
received her. She said, "What happens in your house is more important than
what happens in the White House." And you know she's 100% correct on
that.

Unlike another philosopher, Socrates, I'm going to resist giving you
a lot of free advice. Socrates . . . remember that he used to go around giving
advice to people? And they poisoned him. My favorite advice story is about
another predecessor of mine, Jack Kennedy. President Kennedy, when he
spoke to a group of business people, said, "If I weren't president, I'd be buying stocks right now." A guy in the back said, "Yeah, if you weren't president, I'd be buying stocks right now." So I'm not going to give you any
advice. Alexander may remember this. I used to get advice, and I appreciat-
ed it, just as you've gotten it here from your teachers, just as I expect you've
been privileged to get it all your life from your families.

I got advice from my mother when she was about 90 years old, and
I was President of the United States, after the first helicopter landing I ever
made. You know how you see the helicopter coming in on the South Lawn of
the White House. Barbara and I were coming back from our first visit to
Camp David, and we landed on the South Lawn. I got out of the helicopter
and walked into the diplomatic entrance of the White House. The Chief
Usher, the guy who runs the White House, and does it very, very well indeed,
I might add, said, "Your mother's calling, Sir." I said, "Oh, fine." "George,
I just saw you land. CNN had it live. You landed on the White House lawn.
Isn't that wonderful?" I said, "Oh, it's just great, Mom. You're spoiled to
death when you're president." She said, "But I noticed something." She said,
"I remember how Ronald Reagan would wait at the foot of the stairs of the
helicopter until Nancy came off and then they would go in together." I said,
"Mother, I will never walk ahead of Barbara again." And I didn't. For four
years.

So, three pieces of advice. Take what you've learned here and use it to help others. Treasure the friendships made here, because they're going to last a lifetime. And never neglect family. Robert put it, "Finish up strong." We could throw that in as a piece of advice too. I was President of the United States, but I know what fundamentally matters is your friends, your family and your faith.

*This panel discussion took place on November 7, 1997,
as part of the homecoming program for the Classes of 1948-1959,
hosted by the Language Department.*

THE FUTURE IS UPON US: FORECASTS FROM THE FIELD

*Thomas D. Bloomer '49P, Peter M. Buchanan '53, Erik C. Esselstyn '55,
Samuel A. Hartwell '48, Patricia M. Kelleher '48, John A. Mendelson '58,
Brian A. Rosborough '58P, Porter K. Wheeler '58P*

Brian A. Rosborough '58P, Moderator. Each panelist will speak from the heart about their experience as much as they care or dare, and speculate about the future. First, a classmate, the sort of classmate you used to get off the walk for because he was so impressive, John Mendelson. He will talk a little bit about the market.

John A. Mendelson '58. I'll start with a quick look backward to where we have been over the last ten years. Ten years ago there were approximately 2,100 mutual funds; now there are 6,700. Their assets ten years ago were 850 billion; 4.2 trillion now. Volume on the New York Stock Exchange ten years ago was about 190 million shares; now it's about 550 million. One of the more interesting statistics goes back a little further, to 1965, when approximately 10% of the US population owned stocks, while now that number is around 43%, directly or indirectly.

Another amazing change is in the technology of the business. When I began in the 1960s, runners ran around Wall Street physically delivering securities. Half of them stopped off at bars on the way, so it was a slow and inaccurate process on certain days. Another example: the first job I ever had was on the floor of the New York Stock Exchange in 1960, the summer of my junior year at Princeton. As a clerk, I filled out reports from one of the brokers and put them in pneumatic tubes, which were sent to booths at the end of the exchange. Half of them got stuck in the tubes, and a lot of them had written errors. At the end of the day, I was given a list of 30 or 40 stocks and had to call various brokers for the last sales. Today, we have a home on Lake Champlain and I have a stock machine there where I can get every bit of information in the world. Even this morning I got the stock quotes from

CNBC at the Deerfield Inn. I don't know about you, but I don't remember getting stock quotes at the Deerfield Inn before.

A look ahead: six things strike me. The first is electronic trading. All of our children are computer literate now; I think within ten years you are going to see 80% of all trades done on line; it's going to get much more dramatic. A second factor is international investing, so-called emerging markets. There is going to be a lot more interest in China, Russia, and Eastern Europe. A third factor that looks to me quite close is 24-hour trading. This will drive a number of people, including my wife, crazy. The bond market has been trading 24 hours for some time now; the expression is "pass the book" from New York to Tokyo to London.

A fourth factor is the use of what is known as artificial intelligence to pick stock, using computers or, let's say, non-human brains. Fifth, I would expect to see once again a major change in the players, the stocks we trade, turning over into totally new industries such as software and biotech. Finally, the financial service industry has become one of the dominant parts of American business. I think it fair to say that the financial services industry, the entertainment industry, perhaps some of the technology industries, are in the forefront here. The financial services industry continues to attract very good young people, and I expect it to remain right on the top.

Rosborough. Clearly, these forces will have an impact on employment, what people do. A vast number of people between New Delhi and Vladivostok will enter the middle class in the next 15-20 years. Right now there are 25 million people from OCED countries unemployed and another 50 million under-employed, moving around with plants and animals. It's a very fluid system. Our next panelist has taken a look not at the middle where we are all productively employed, but at inner city work forces and the struggle there to find meaningful work. Sam Hartwell is a multi-engine pilot, a mountain climber, and a nonprofit entrepreneur who founded the East Harlem employment service known as Strive.

Samuel A. Hartwell '48. I made a pass through Deerfield and Princeton, hardly knowing what was going on in either place. Now I find myself in the middle of a tornado called Welfare to Work, and the reason is that twelve years ago I co-founded an employment agency in Harlem, which is now in six cities, New York, Pittsburgh, Chicago, Boston, Philadelphia and Baltimore. We are placing about 3,000 people a year in jobs.

The kind of people we deal with are as close to the unemployable as we can get. Who are they? People with marginal education, no work history, and very little familiarity with what is required in a professional environment. Many of them have an attitude problem, born of very rough treatment in schools, at home and on the street. We cannot deal with people who are over a certain line, those who are drug addicted or emotionally unstable or irretrievably hostile and unresponsive to guidance.

The entry level jobs that we get for these clients of ours are at $7, $8 and $9 an hour. We put them in such august Fortune 500 companies as Morgan Stanley, Merrill Lynch, IBM, AT&T, and so on. And now, believe it or not, we have been on "60 Minutes" and we've been down to the White House by invitation and to Harvard (which I also passed through).

We have a three-week training program that costs us about $1,500 a client. Our job retention rate is 80%. As someone said, if you catch a wave, ride it as far as you can, and that's what we are doing. The one thing I have learned out of all of this is that the so-called disadvantaged inner city young adults are not all that disadvantaged. They are intelligent and motivated, and they have energy. It is amazing how little help they need to become valuable employees, financially independent individuals, responsible parents. I truly believe this.

We follow up the placement of a client, sometimes calling after the very first day of work. If that person is fired or quits, we ask him or her to come back to Strive for a counseling session, and re-place the person in work. Twenty to forty percent of our graduates are actually re-placed, some two, three or four times before we give up. That's the reason our retention rates are so high. Government programs don't have this element, and they should.

People come to us for all kinds of reasons. The men who are in the drug trade come to get away from it; that's a dangerous trade, a boring trade. Ex-prisoners come because they don't want to go back to prison, and are looking for a way to function normally. Some of the women are trying to get away from living with a mother, or from being at home with the children. Almost all of them are trying to get away from something. They see Strive as an avenue to independence.

We lose about 10-20% of each class, and another 10-20% after graduation. So we have a large attrition rate, and we don't have all the answers. Some people are just not motivated to work, and some have so much hostility that they cannot get rid of it.

So, as far as forecasting the future, I think that Welfare to Work will in fact work. At Strive we are not the only ones; there other people doing what we are doing. People on welfare want to work and become valuable citizens.

Rosborough. Fourteen members of the Bloomer family have come through this place. Tom is going to tell us a little bit about telecommunications, one of the drivers of change, and about the velocity of change, with a perspective on how students might come together in telecommunications in the next few years.

Thomas D. Bloomer '49P. Telecommunications is such a broad topic that I struggled to think how to personalize it and draw it down to our collective experience at Deerfield. My own story actually began with Deerfield, which for me was an enabler. Deerfield enabled me to leave a small rural town in upstate New York and get into Dartmouth, which in turn led to Harvard Business School, and then to a special assignment in the Army, where I was introduced to data and information processing forty years ago.

After three years in the Army, I was hired by IBM and sent to be a salesman at the Pentagon. Much like the stock runners that John described, the Army at that time kept their records on the Reserve and the National Guard with a quill pen. For the mobilization at that time for the Bay of Pigs, they couldn't mobilize the reserves with pen and pencil, so they really had to use punch cards. The system was about half installed and kind of chaotic; we even mobilized a few veterans of the Spanish American War from the Veterans' Hospitals.

My thesis connects telecommunications to the bonding experience here at Deerfield. It relates to experience I had at Dartmouth on the alumni council, in charge of the communications committee. Kids who go to Dartmouth have to have a computer as they walk in the door. It is mandatory that they are connected to the Dartmouth Net and through that to the Internet. They use the system for research and to write papers, but basically the largest use is to communicate with their friends, professors, and family. Use of the telephone has gone down dramatically. When these students graduate, what do you do, turn off the e-mail and the Internet connection?

Now overlay that experience on Deerfield. Last year, they wired the buildings; this year, there are computers in the rooms and students can get on the Internet. Soon they will have e-mail. Deerfield students in the very near future will be utilizing the computer as much as they do in colleges. What are we going to do when they graduate? Turn off their connections?

When I left Deerfield, I felt that I had built strong bonds with many friends. Now, through Deerfield's facilitation of email, the bonds will remain strong. Our task is to work with technology within the institution to take advantage of the advancements that are clearly possible today. I believe that technology enhances normal communications, that the potential far outweighs the risks.

Rosborough. Our next speaker, Porter Wheeler, will talk about the whole issue of how we will move around in the next few years, how goods and people are going to be mobile in the next generation.

Porter K. Wheeler '58P. I think that mobility in the US in terms of both people and goods has been one of the keys to our economic and social success. I want to highlight quickly a few major changes and then talk a little about where I see this in the future.

When we were here in the 50s there existed no interstate highway system, no jet planes except in the military, and no double stack container system. Not all the changes have been in a positive direction. I think we all remember going up to the Deerfield station and catching a train at vacation time. Rail passenger service has suffered major financial and service withdrawals and we are frankly in somewhat of a crisis at the moment. The rail freight industry did increase its productivity and has now begun to show a few signs of strain in the West. We may also have some strain in the East after some of the mega-mergers currently being considered.

Throughout all this, our mobility, our ability to move goods and people, has been extremely high and has progressed well. We are beginning to hit boundaries on that, small trouble spots. Vehicle miles traveled by automobiles have grown; congestion on the highways is becoming pervasive, a real economic burden. Freight is moving faster and more cheaply, but I think the railroads have pretty much exhausted their ability to reduce cost and increase capacity. We are a little bit that way too in the highway system.

Where are we going to go? I frankly think that the infrastructure has exhausted its base of support at the federal level. If you want major improvements, they basically have to involve private capital and some quasi-privatization or public-private partnership. I see a big trend there. Secondly, I see a number of aspects of technology coming in. It is being done right now through electronic information such as electronic train control. One of the simplest devices is the cell phone where people are in immediate contact with any source of information they want. I think you will see this become more routine and be used to speed traffic flows.

In the past few weeks we have seen a couple of positive things, where we are hitting some boundaries on energy use and emission from automobiles. We have seen zero emission vehicles announced. Again, fuel cells look very promising as the coming power source. In personal vehicles, remarkable improvements have been made both in energy efficiency and emissions. But we see both good and bad there, because a very large part of the new fleet consists of vans or sport utility vehicles, which are less fuel efficient and emit more particulates and more CO_2. Technology is where I am looking to find the breakthroughs.

Rosborough. Our next speaker, Erik Esselstyn, has had a lifetime commitment to reducing the human impact on the land, in his own words leaving a gentler footprint, and perhaps this came from walking behind plows on the family farm all those years. There he saw with his own eyes the impact of DDT on the reduction of biological life, so much so that in 1992 he took a master's in environmental studies and started his own institution, Cross Creek Initiative.

Erik C. Esselstyn '55. When we first used DDT in the main dairy barn, the flies disappeared and so did the butterflies, and the bluebirds and Baltimore orioles. As I grew up and left the farm, the land was increasingly leased to people who began to use advanced herbicides and pesticides. I can remember once going back and going out to one of the most fertile pieces of the land, 54 acres of absolutely flat tableland where we raised corn and wheat when I was a kid. I dug up a couple of wheelbarrows of sod to bring to the lawn across from the house where I grew up, because my stepmother was repairing some lawn around her flower bed, and she wanted some good soil for it. The long and short of the story is that that soil wouldn't grow grass seed for about five years.

That was the beginning of a wake-up call for me and my going to the Yale School of Forestry in my fifties, simply trying to put a professional foundation under a lot of concern and care about what is going on in the planet. I too have waited in lines of traffic; I too have been to Los Angeles and felt my eyes smart; I have chewed the air in Mexico City and in parts of Africa and Central America. What are we going to do about it?

I like to teach with metaphors. The two biggest issues that the kids at Deerfield will deal with are most closely related to population and climate change. To use an old African proverb, the planet is not ours, it is given to us in trust for future generations. From this morning's panel we learned that the Deerfield community had a profound influence on all of us. Pulling words from the panel, I learned that the community is stable and increasingly diverse, that it honors women and has a willingness to risk. To quote Eric Widmer, "We would be foolhardy, wrongheaded, if we sought to increase the size of the school." I would ask everyone to tell me why the planet Earth at this point is any different from Deerfield. Are we perhaps foolhardy and wrongheaded if we think we can continue to grow as we have in the past?

What was exciting about the description of the Deerfield community was that it is not growing physically at all, but it is developing and enriching itself, becoming more diverse, more complex, more rich, and more able to serve the community, not because it is growing but because it is stable. I think it is time for the planet and the human species to focus more on enriching itself in many ways, for example, in art and in honoring women, than on physical growth.

The aspirations of people are being driven by what America has. Three summers ago I was at a bar in a little community in Mali in Central Africa. People who were dragging in firewood from the fields would stop at the door of this place and watch "Baywatch," in the middle of Africa. We are 5% of the world population, and someone said this morning that the people who can afford to go to Deerfield represent 3% of that 5%. Most of us sit, I think, in the midst of a society something akin to that of Tutankhamen's, in terms of privilege and access to medical care, technology, friends, connections, creature comforts and a very comfortable retirement plan. I think that the same things that have driven much of our success can drive many of our solutions to the problems of climate change and population.

Rosborough.   Pat Kelleher knew you when you had hair. No wonder, because her father was the barber here. She followed her father and his three sisters to Deerfield. If you think of the environment, education is probably the biggest environmental problem, and Pat has devoted her life to education.

Patricia M. Kelleher '48.   Almost every day that you pick up the paper, there is an article about education, with pros and cons. It is a major issue in the public sector: that's where the tax dollars go. It seems as if in the public system they run around to find a new thing to change, when I think you need to stand still and look to see where you are coming from. When I began in the public system in the early 60s, we had good strong schools. I think a lot of it got away from us in the 60s through a lack of authority and a departure from traditional kinds of education. The courts did not back up administrators.

How do you turn it around? Often the public schools look toward us private schools. Both the private schools and Catholic schools have maintained success, have a high percentage of graduates. Catholic schools do very well in the inner city, perhaps because we have retained the structure and look at the dignity of each student. For instance, there is a lot to be said about dressing properly as we had to do here at Deerfield. It affects the whole atmosphere of a school. When a teacher is distracted by the way students are dressed, it affects the whole lesson plan.

For the future, we are looking into different ways of teaching students, into multiple intelligences and varying learning styles. Block scheduling is also a hot topic right now. One of the things I learned at Deerfield was Frank Boyden's philosophy of education, the way he treated each person as an individual. I don't think he used the expression, "Win-win," but he gave the opportunity for people to bail out of a tight situation. I often use this story: a Deerfield student left campus and went to the train station, to go down to Northampton to see a girlfriend at Smith. The headmaster let it happen, and then he drove to the train station and got there before the train. The young man got off, and Mr. Boyden went over to him and said, "Were you looking for a ride back to Deerfield?" If you back kids into a corner, they come out fighting. If you give them a chance to say, "Yes, I made a mistake but you are recognizing me as a real person," it is a great way of approaching discipline.

When you talk about changes and new types of teaching and technology, you are really going back and saying, we need the structure. Youngsters need to know there are certain things you do on a regular basis, which include caring about where they are and what they are doing.

Rosborough. Peter Buchanan wants to talk to us briefly about the role of philanthropy, seed capital, and social investment in education, and to see how we might get involved in that sport.

Peter M. Buchanan '53. Having spent more than two thirds of my professional life in philanthropy and support of education, I am still not certain what philanthropy is, but I am very certain about what it means. Hoping that many of you will not know all of the following descriptors of American philanthropy, I thought they should precede any predictions.

The Internal Revenue Service, which openly admits it cannot screen the thousands of applications it receives for tax exempt status every year, tells us that there are approximately 600,000 charitable organizations, including some 260,000 religious organizations. In the charitable numbers are also 49,000 human services organizations, 27,000 health agencies, 18,000 educational institutions and 15,000 cultural groups, among many others of more modest size.

Of the adult population of approximately 190 million people, about

50%, or 95 million, volunteer and about 86 million make a contribution to charity each year, a participation rate of about 45%, the envy of the world. From all sources, the tax exempt organizations receive an estimated 144 billion dollars, or roughly 2% of the gross domestic product. Giving is extraordinarily dependent on the economic health of the nation, as well as on changes in the tax code.

Making predictions violates one of my favorite admonitions: a closed mouth gathers no feet. Notwithstanding that, here are a few predictions about what will or will not happen in American philanthropy. First, the charitable deduction taken away in the 1986 tax law will never be restored. Second, virtually all annual gifts will be solicited, sent, and acknowledged electronically, with much face to face interaction on the screen. Third, the share of giving between and among religion, education, human services and health will probably remain virtually unchanged, but the giving to each will significantly exceed the rate of inflation as government support declines.

Fourth, the majority of Americans will make their gifts to investment or other financial service companies for subsequent designation to charities of their choice. Fifth, women will give more to charity than men will. Sixth, someone in this room will live to see a 100 billion dollar gift in the tradition of Annenberg, Turner, and a hopefully more generous Gates. Seventh, Deerfield will be the first secondary school on the planet to successfully complete a billion dollar campaign. Coming full circle, the oft-quoted epitaph in this field still captures the spirit of what we know as philanthropy: "What I spent is gone. What I kept is lost, but what I gave to charity will be mine forever." Deerfield is surely ours.

John Louis Dormitory, 1998

Photograph - Gabriel Amadeus Cooney
Deerfield Academy Archives
Deerfield, Massachusetts

V. The Global Journey.

Other speakers joined Alice and Warren Ilchman in urging
Deerfield to extend its scope still more widely into the world.
The school not only provides a paradigm for principled decision-
making in adult life, but also serves as an institutional model for
educational excellence in the international arena.

Rick Barton gave this talk on April 19, 1997,
at the homecoming for the Classes of 1960-1968,
hosted by the English Department.

TAKING DEERFIELD TO THE ENDS OF THE EARTH

Frederick D. Barton '67

TODAY'S HIGH SCHOOL STUDENTS probably don't think much about the ways that their school experience will affect them in later life. Now, however, 30 years after my own graduation, I have gained a little insight into the ways that Deerfield Academy has influenced me over time. I realize that many aspects of my work emulate what I found at Deerfield, even though the school world seems poles away from the beleaguered societies that USAID serves. It is revealing to examine that work in the light of a small country boarding school for boys, run by a headmaster who retired in 1968 after 66 years on the job, and staffed by a collection of sometimes eccentric teachers who dedicated their lives to the place around the clock.

In looking at my work, it is in fact possible to connect the unique and indigenous Deerfield model to those communities which have eaten away at themselves, have destroyed each other, and have very little left. We try to find such a model, to encourage it to grow, to see if we can give people the attitudes that will allow democracy to take hold in the future.

The construct that I have used over the years has three critical elements, as does the Deerfield paradigm. The first is that there must be a clear sense of direction, a vision. For Deerfield it has always been that the students come first, that the institution is never greater than its individual members. In our work we apply the same principle. As I'll describe, we spend a lot of time looking for the ordinary people and their thoughts and hopes.

The second element is building a team and empowering its members. At Deerfield, the team was every one of us. Each had important responsibilities and roles. You would hear about not only the great varsity star but also the efforts of a freshman in second soccer, conveying a sense that each of us was vital to the health of the larger organization. In our work, we apply this principle by finding people who are builders and organizers, who want to nourish the capacities of the local citizens. We look for those who value the local folks for their wisdom, rather than turning to us.

The third element of our efforts is our attempt to communicate all the time. By this I refer to the great communication of role modeling, which at Deerfield was so powerful. Frank Boyden, the Headmaster, was a clear example of that, in his way of providing a constant connection with us; for instance coming on the squawk box and saying, "Now, boys, I want you all to go to the window and look at the colors of the hills." I never thought of Frank Boyden as a great naturalist, but that image sticks with me. Today's Headmaster too comes down to the field and talks to the teams or goes up on stage to congratulate the performers.

I think of our teachers, Bryce Lambert, who in retirement still compliments me when I write a good piece for the Maine paper he reads; or the late Bob Crow with his quack theories, his great theses that the beaches should be free or that Herbert Hoover was one of our most underestimated presidents. And of course Bob Merriam's loving desire that all of us would have a haircut like his own.

I mustn't be too idealistic about the models, however. Another part of our Deerfield heritage was to question authority, a critical approach as we go into these brutally tough places, where authority has defined itself in a way that works against the interests of the people. I remember a young teacher, David Morine {'62}, whom Frank Boyden had perhaps taken on to make sure he didn't later end up with a record only a president could pardon. David started a sort of sneak attack war with us in our senior winter, which helped that term go faster. He would jump out of a garbage pail with a snowball or be hiding with one behind a building. It was my job one day to tour for the admissions office a much-desired tennis player recruit. When I brought him back to my room, there was Dave Morine standing with two snowballs. I threw my coat over him and David stood there and melted down for the next twenty minutes.

Another authority-questioning figure I remember was my classmate Mike Percy. In school meetings, he would get as close as possible to the Headmaster without being seen. He had a little high-pitched whistle, and just as the Headmaster would get the room quieted down, he would blow that whistle. Thinking that the squeal was his hearing aid, Mr. Boyden would pretty quickly tune himself right out of the room. To shake up our unseasoned floor master, Mike brought a radio set back with him from a vacation and set up a little radio station in his room. He would tune the master's radio to that frequency and broadcast to the poor man's bedside his impersonation of the Headmaster's voice reading collections of off-color literature.

Of course there were elements of school life that were not as healthy: there was excessive conformity at times, some bullying, a sense of entitlement. But all in all, it was a dynamic community. I would like to turn to the work we do in some of our far-flung places, to describe how some of that dynamism applies there.

During the post-Cold War period, at any one time over the last decade, 25 wars have been going on. Many of the tools that we have for dealing with these circumstances are tools of the Cold War: apolitical aid, taking care of emergencies. For example, we can stabilize Goma, Zaire, with a million new residents arriving within a two-week period; we can control the cholera epidemic; we can provide food and water. We are ensuring essential survival, certainly no more than that.

At the other end is sustainable development, building economies and democratic systems. While these projects too have become relatively sophisticated, much of that work has been overtaken by the onset of these wars, these conflict emergencies. Rwanda, for example, was considered a sustainable development success story, because it had an effective AIDS control program, coffee exports programs and other indications that the country was going to be a future economic force in central Africa. People didn't see that the political fabric was unraveling dramatically. There is certainly a need for a new political tool to intervene in some of these countries.

At the same time, we have a dwindling foreign aid situation, where the US is the third largest gross contributor of foreign aid in the world but only about the 25th per capita. We spend about $7 billion worldwide, half of which goes to Egypt and Israel. Another billion is for emergency surplus food, leaving about $2.5 billion as our pool of resources. From the old image of the carrot and the stick, we now have a powerful, daunting stick at our disposal, which we must use with caution, and a tiny pre-scrubbed supermarket carrot. Therefore we have tried to create a small, fast, direct political development office for countries emerging from distress. We have worked in these first years chiefly in emerging societies such as Bosnia, Haiti, Rwanda, Liberia, Angola, Sri Lanka and Guatemala.

Our department is a small firm that tries to use a venture capital model. In fact, our resource pool is not much greater than that of Deerfield Academy. As a result, we must try to be catalytic in every way. The first thing is to review a situation to see if it is of significance to the United States. Is there a political opening, a peace accord, a cease fire, an election that suggests a change in atmospherics? We have to find the people who can express themselves. In Sarajevo in June, 1994, I had a wonderful translator, who was extremely literal. When, during the sniping, I said, "Why would anyone want to have children under these circumstances?" she said, "We will go to the maternity ward." There I had what I consider as one of my career moments: the doctor, with less sense of privacy than we have in the West, took me in to interview a woman in labor, while she was delivering a child.

If we asked about fundamentalist women's organizations, or the front line, or the lives of children, we would visit the places where those activities were happening. By the time you have had one-on-one meetings with a hundred people, you have an incredibly valuable weight of evidence. You simply need to cover the prime minister and the political leaders, the usual suspects, in the first couple of days and then go to the people. In Sarajevo, for instance, we came back with the view that, despite the cease fire, the opening was not real, and we would be premature trying to get in then.

A big trick of venture capitalism is to say no. What we discovered in Liberia was very much the same thing. We met the fighters in Tubmanberg and outside of Buchanan. On the average they are about seventeen and a half years old; they have a dependent, usually a child; they look as if they are on drugs; they have no other skills; their leadership is nonexistent. It seems as if Mad Max and the Lord of the Flies got together and had offspring, and you recognize that only something close to a miracle will create a successful intervention. In fact, Liberia taught me a little bit about caution.

We had been blithely out there meeting with these folks and with General Ruth, a sort of housemother out in the bush. The United Nations showed up a couple of weeks after we'd left with a helicopter. Her boys took the helicopter hostage, and sent the UN officials off in their underwear and two other representatives away with no clothing at all. Thus the weight of evidence was against an opportunity there. We try to use a problem-solving model that accepts that 80% solutions at the right time are more valuable than a perfected plan.

One case history gives a good sense of our work. Haiti is a little bit more promising, despite all the work it still has to do. In 1990, there was a breakthrough, an honest election, the first ever in Haiti, won by a rather simple figure, a bright and clever man, the priest Bertrand Aristide. He won with the most honest promise I have ever heard a politician make, the reason, I suspect, that he got 80% of the vote. The promise was that he would take Haiti from misery to poverty with dignity. After several hundred years of raw exploitation in every sense of the people and the earth, that was a brave new day.

As somebody once told me, all Haiti needs is a new military class, a new political class, and a new economic class. It is amazing that over the last couple of years, two of the three have been pretty well established and have brought dignity to the people. The United States military intervention has provided a shield so that the process could unfold. We felt that the system of intimidation was at the core of the society's inability to develop, and that system depended on enforcement by the Haitian military. When President Aristide decided to disband the military and turn their headquarters over to a newly created ministry of women, he opened the opportunity for something closer to a transforming initiative than anything I'll have a chance to do.

We took the Haitian military, 5,000 of perhaps 7,000 soldiers, and put them through a vocational retraining program, giving them the initial tools for joining the society. It was a basic civilization program and essentially got these people out of play, changing their influence on society and giving them something of a start. Even though the Haitian economy will take forever to get going again, the home construction and road construction businesses are very much underway.

Our second undertaking was to find the 70% of the population that lived outside of Port-au-Prince. One of the difficulties with international assistance is that it comes into the central capital and runs into a nonexistent system for dispersal, with no real capacity for getting out into the society. We set up thirteen offices all around the country, staffed with people who had good experience in international work, community organizing or political organizing, and we said to them: "Find and fund almost any initiative that you can in the local community that has great local participation, where they are willing to have open decision-making and to handle their finances in a transparent way. We don't care what you do, whether it's schools or water systems; just stimulate the basic desire that we think exists out there."

In Haiti there was a tremendous pent-up demand to get on with their lives, along with expectations for the new day coming with Aristide. As a result, over the last year and a half, we have built or rebuilt about 600 schools, been involved in about 114 of the 131 communities, and started to give people a sense that it is their own future, that they can take responsibility, that someone will be there to partner with them. We were able to take a group of new mayors and give them an opportunity to do something for their constituents. When we went back, it was encouraging to see just how sophisticated the new group of public officials had become in packaging programs, soliciting funds, and delivering something to their people, a previously nonexistent achievement in Haiti as in most other countries where we work.

Essentially what we are trying to do is help people move beyond war, beyond a punitive system of intimidation, toward basic freedoms of movement, speech and assembly. It is pre-democracy work. Even though these stories are hopeful, one might wonder why we bother to do this; why not make America one more gated community? We "bother" for the same reason that the Deerfield community model works, not just because of the mission, the team and the communications, but because Deerfield has always been part of the larger world. Our school community mattered only as part of this region, nation and world. Otherwise, we would have become just one more precious, elite place of little relevance elsewhere. It is clear that people at Deerfield continue to make the dynamic choice, to care for each other, to trust each other, and to work together for a common purpose. What a fortunate heritage.

Malcolm McKenzie presented these remarks as a participant in the panel,
"Educational Vistas Ahead," part of "The School's Program for Our Alumni"
during the Grand Celebration weekend, October 3, 1998.

GOING GLOBAL

Malcolm McKenzie

LET ME BEGIN BY STATING SOMETHING OBVIOUS. It is a great pleasure and privilege for me to be here this weekend. I have already enjoyed hugely the past day and a half, and I know that the rest of today and tomorrow morning will be as enjoyable. I want now to make a second point that is also obvious. I hope that not everything else I say will be quite so obvious!

An obvious characteristic of educational institutions is that they change people who teach and learn in them. That is one of the wonderful, often unspoken, joys of teaching. Of course, great institutions change people all the time, in ways large and small. After only a day and a half here this weekend, I have noticed some deep shifts in my image and concept of this academy. I am changed as a consequence. I was particularly affected by some of the insights offered us so generously by the Ilchmans last night. Their comments about national schools and global schools really did get me thinking.

I came here to share some thoughts, as a relative outsider, about Deerfield on the global high school stage. My topic has not altered, but the thoughts have. So I shall not offer you the prepared speech which slumbers on my computer. What I give you now is fresh-baked, early this morning. I hope that it is not half-baked. I trust that the dough is rising, or, even better, has risen.

Ladies and Gentlemen, do you know that beyond this valley, right now, out there, are about 1,000 schools worldwide that call themselves International Schools, with a capital "I" and a capital "S"? They all claim to offer an International Education, again with a capital "I" and this time a capital "E". My school, Maru a Pula, I hasten to add, is not one of these. Many of these schools follow the programme of the International Baccalaureate Organisation. For some decades the IBO has offered the International

Baccalaureate, a rigorous and exciting curriculum for the last two years of high school. It now provides, in addition, a middle years programme and an elementary school course. It is K through 12 and avowedly international. It is worth noting that other schools which do not self-style themselves International nevertheless also offer the IB programme.

What makes an International School international? What does such a school look and feel like? What product does an International Education offer? What sort of student is its outcome?

In a chapter that I was recently commissioned to write for a book on perspectives in International Education, I analysed the use of the word "international" in the statement of aims of the IBO. This statement is a one-page, three-paragraph document that uses the word "international" exactly five times, each time with a different meaning. I remember from my years of studying philosophy a wonderful phrase used by Wittgenstein, where he speaks of the "bewitchment of intelligence by language." I have no doubt that, in our application of the word "international" to education, we have allowed our intelligences to become bewitched, or perhaps bewizarded, by language.

One thing that has become clear to me, the more I have researched this topic, is that an education that is truly international (lower case "i") is not necessarily the prerogative of International Schools. What is so important, and what we should be trying to develop in such an education, is an attitude of mind. We are talking about the movement across frontiers and geographical boundaries of ideas and values, not simply people and places, and the growth of a mindset in our teachers and students that encapsulates this.

Let me suggest some of the values and ideas that must be at the heart of an international education. Our students and teachers must become world-minded and also open-minded. It is no good possessing a global consciousness which shows you that the world is your oyster, if all that you are concerned about is the exploitation of pearls. We must develop a sense of individual and cultural self-esteem, and these must be concomitant. We must promote a feeling of global interdependence and a commitment to world peace and development. Community service learning and environmental and experiential study programmes have a real input here. Viewed from this perspective, it is indeed the case that schools that are national schools, or at least schools that do not proclaim themselves International Schools, can readily deliver an education that is international or global in the knowledge, awareness and ability to act of its students.

What is Deerfield Academy doing about this? How is it locating itself within this major movement across the world in 20th century high school education?

I can comment on only one aspect of this from within Deerfield. I was invited to the NAIS Annual Conference in Washington in 1996 to be part of a panel discussion on Internationalism in Education, coordinated by Peter Pelham. About forty schools participated in this workshop, from which "Global Connections," as it has come to be called, was born. Three key members of this group, all of which were represented from the outset, are Deerfield Academy, Maru a Pula, and the Geelong Grammar School near Melbourne, Australia. A primary focus at this early stage is to explore how national schools with interests in global networks and international trends in education can operate to mutual benefit within a loose federation or consortium. We believe that we have found an uncharted niche in the growing market of associations of schools by targeting national schools that have international aspirations.

Global Connections sprang from this initial Washington workshop. We held our first full conference at St. Stithian's School in Johannesburg and Maru a Pula in February 1997. In March this year we moved to the Geelong Grammar School near Melbourne and SCEGGS Redlands in Sydney. There are already about 70 high schools in the group. We have been assembling fine national schools, of different types, all deeply rooted in themselves and their contexts, all the centres of their universes, as Deerfield is so clearly, but all determined to enrich themselves by finding out more about the periphery and the circumference. In 1999 we shall meet at Wellington College in England. The theme of that gathering is Leadership and Team Building, which we shall uncover in a hands-on, practical manner. In this light, it was interesting to hear Kerry Emanuel speak yesterday of ways of solving global problems appropriate to the coming century. Our millennial meeting is planned for Deerfield, and then we hope to be hosted in Asia the following year. By that stage we shall have visited most of the major continents of the earth!

The issues and themes to which we are dedicating ourselves are the following: the value of community service and its place in an education that is truly international; the importance of environmental and conservation learning that is experiential in nature; the relationship between advantaged and less advantaged schools and how they might work in symbiotic partnerships; exchanges of students and faculty through swaps and other visits; using technology in our schools, both information and other, that is appropriate to our needs and to our world; and, finally, what globalisation in education means, exactly. This group of national high schools worldwide has the potential to become a significant world educational force and it is wonderful that Deerfield is at its forefront.

One question to be asked of Deerfield's involvement with this group is: what does the academy have to offer to fellow travellers in different parts of the world? I ask this question first, largely because it is appropriate to place it there when community service features so clearly on our agenda. Its corollary is to enquire what Deerfield has to gain. I could give you my answers regarding those gifts that Deerfield has to offer, but I won't now, as this seems to me to be a task for your students and faculty to engage with first. It is certainly proper to assess what you have to offer, not just what you might gain. Yet your school will gain, at the very least, the following:

Opportunities for school-to-school partnerships worldwide; further opportunities to make friends and influence people, something which everyone outside America takes to be your national pastime, after sport; chances for students and faculty to travel, to find out, and to bring back insights into your already rich curriculum; possibilities for current and recently graduated students to engage in environmental and community service vacation programmes worldwide; membership in a global network; finally, and perhaps most important, an enhanced capacity to see yourselves as others see you. This last point is, for me, vital. Going global is, yes, about discovering exotic places and exotic foods. It is also about enrolling exotic students and employing exotic faculty in our schools. But it is, at a fundamental level, about much more than that.

There is a famous legend about a place on the Cherwell River in Oxford called Parsons' Pleasure. There, so the story goes, male Fellows and Dons were allowed to bathe naked. This retreat is set back from the main channel and therefore beyond the gaze of female eyes as they punt elegantly down the river. One day, we are told, a group of adventurous female undergraduates decided to take the side channel to see what they might see. Imagine the shock and horror of the discreet and perhaps prudish teachers, caught with their pants down. Four of them leapt up and pulled on their trousers hurriedly: the fifth, in more contemplative and philosophical fashion, pulled his trousers over his head. The punt glided by, the danger of discovery receded, and the four rounded upon their colleague.

"What on earth possessed you to do that?"

Came the reply: "I don't know how you gentlemen are recognised around Oxford, but people know me by my face."

The real point of my oppidan legend, of course, is that there are very few of us who know accurately how others see and identify us. The truth is that we are seen through the obvious face that we present to them. Yet we know that our obvious face is often unfamiliar to us—the unexpected, side-long glance in the mirror never seems true to us; the voice captured on tape always seems stilted when it belongs to us. Becoming global in our perspective is a fine way to overcome this, to get to know ourselves better and more truly through the mirror of cultural and other difference. Difference, that great educator, gives us self-knowledge and makes us as a consequence more perceptive about our own domestic challenges and more able to carry on the business of our backyard. Going global makes the local make more sense.

In seizing this initiative, Deerfield Academy is doing something that few of your compatriot peers have considered seriously. I am sure that, by becoming better connected globally, you will become even more deeply rooted than you already are in the fertile soils of this valley, and more truly able to fulfill your mission as an American school in a global context.

*Meera Viswanathan offered these thoughts at the conclusion of the homecoming weekend
for the Classes of 1948-1959, hosted by the Language Department.
Her remarks followed two presentations. The first was a talk by Ann Kerr W'49,
"The Role of Deerfield in our Lives and Our Outlooks."
In it, Mrs. Kerr reflected on the experiences of her late husband Malcolm '49
as president of the American University in Beirut and her own life since his assassination,
and then read from her book,* Come with Me from Lebanon.
*Her talk was followed by remarks from John Waterbury '57, President-elect of the American
University in Beirut, shortly before he left for Lebanon to begin his work there.*

HOMEWARD BOUND

Meera S. Viswanathan H'95

THE NOTION OF JOURNEYS AND OF TRAVEL ties together many of our celebra-
tions. This weekend was made possible by the journeys of all of you who have
traveled from your distant homes. We have had the marvelous recounting of
Ann Kerr's voyage as she read from her book, *Come with Me from Lebanon*—
surely because of Ann the voice of the turtledove is heard in the Deerfield
Valley once again. We have heard about the prospective voyage of John
Waterbury as he sets out for the presidency of the American University in
Beirut. Our hearts go with him as we think and marvel that in this world,
where there is so much cynicism and a kind of jaded enervation, people
should still possess idealism and belief in simple principles.

I am reminded also that one of the courses that I most enjoy teaching at Brown is one entitled "Travel and Tourism through the Ages." In it,
we read many works from the genre of travel literature, ranging from Marco
Polo's account of China and Central Asia in the 13th century, to John
Bunyan's seventeenth century allegory *Pilgrim's Progress*, to more modern narratives as well. I am struck by the way most voyages fall into one of two categories. One is the voyage of youth, which more often than not is linear, a
voyage from here to there, sometimes of acquisition but certainly of explo-
ration, its goal to search out new things. It's a voyage in which the love of
home often remains, but really it's the passion for the unknown, the unfamiliar, that propels it. Our Deerfield seniors, I can tell you, are barely able
to contain themselves in anticipation of that voyage out that will commence

for them next June.

It interests me to compare this journey of youth with the voyage of later life, which is invariably one of homecoming, often after a period of exile. It's a voyage which is circular in nature. What one finds is not discovery of the new, but a confirmation of what one always knew in one's heart (the plot of *The Wizard of Oz*, for example). Robert Frost may tell us that "home is where they have to take you in," but if home is a constant, we as voyagers have surely changed. Hence is homecoming especially a voyage of nostalgia, a word derived from the Greek, which means "the pain of return." It is that bittersweet quality that we do not appreciate in youth but in later life come to recognize as extraordinarily precious. It brings us back to Deerfield, for example. A balance of experiences, both shared and solitary, ebbing in and waning outward, brings us together.

This notion of traveling is in fact very exciting and is in some ways what we try to do in education. One other difference between that voyage of youth and the voyage of later life is that in the first the focus is always on the telos, the goal, whereas in later life we realize that it is the process that we are after. The goal may come—think of it as a point on the horizon which beckons us—but that process of getting there is what education is fundamentally about. We aim for our students to follow their own trajectories in this world, and we are trying to prepare them for that world in their travels through Deerfield.

As a good Hindu, I will end with an allusion to the Bible. One line that reverberates within me is Ruth's response to her mother-in-law Naomi, "Whither thou goest I will go." So too does the legacy of Deerfield say to each of us, "Whither thou goest I will go." For Deerfield will always be your home, both what you have brought here and what you will take with you on your journey. May the spirit of Deerfield, that buoyant heartsease, go with Ann back to California and with John forward to Lebanon. Where they go, at least in spirit we go as well. Peace to you and safe journeys.

This panel discussion took place on October 2, 1998,
during the Grand Celebration weekend, as part of
"The Alumni Program for Our School."

THROUGH A LOOKING GLASS BRIGHTLY:
PERSPECTIVES ON A CHANGING WORLD

Frederick D. Barton '67, Kerry A. Emanuel '73, Carrie E. Freeman '92, M. Dozier Gardner '51, Dwayne A. Gathers '80, Gilbert M. Grosvenor '49, Warren Zimmermann '52

Frederick D. Barton '67, Moderator. We have a challenge, in that we have to describe the dynamism of the world, capture its opportunities, stimulate your vision, provoke your comments and questions and engage everybody in the conversation. Even for a group as talented as this, the world is a large challenge. So we've decided to break it up into three sessions. The first will focus on macro-political matters, the second on global concerns, and the third on financial issues. Our first panelists, Warren Zimmermann and Dwayne Gathers, are going to look at the changing face of politics— alliances, coalitions, governments, in other words, geo-politics.

Warren Zimmermann '52. I racked my brains to see what I could remember about my time at Deerfield that had geo-political significance, and I came up with three things. You can recall I was a graduate in 1952, and the early 50s were a period of the beginning of the Cold War, the great match-up between the United States and the Soviet Union. It was also the time of the Korean War, and I can recall that when General MacArthur was fired for insubordination by President Truman, his farewell speech in which he uttered the memorable words, "Old soldiers never die, they just fade away," was piped into the Deerfield dining hall. We also debated the issue of whether Red China, as it was called in those days, should be admitted to the United Nations, and nobody on either the Forum or Senate Debating Team wanted to debate on the side of China. And finally, thanks to the film producer David O. Selznick having two sons at Deerfield, we got the American premiere of that great Cold War thriller, *The Third Man* with Orson Wells, which was all about the division of Vienna into Communist and free parts.

In those days of course, the United States was the leader of the free world. We had faced the Russians down in Berlin, had devised the Marshall Plan to aid the Europeans, and Point Four to help all the developing countries of the world, and had helped to found NATO. We were the power that used our nuclear force to withstand Soviet aggression. I think it's fair to say that the United States in those days showed integrity, leadership and the judicious use of power. The Cold War concluded quite appropriately—where it had begun—with Germany; with the brilliant feat of statesmanship by the United States, Russia and Germany in bringing about the reunification of Germany without a shot being fired, without a person being killed.

Now we're of course at the end of the Cold War and new challenges face us. Issues have become more complex: ethnic conflicts all around the world, the challenge of small and weak countries that can still humiliate us, like Iraq, and global issues like the environment, population, and so forth.

So how is the United States responding to these issues? I have to say I think we're responding quite badly. We ducked the challenges of Bosnia and Rwanda. We pulled our forces out of Somalia when 18 Rangers were killed there. We have been hesitant to almost a criminal degree in Kosovo, where genocide is going on. We remained aloof from a land mines treaty designed to ban one of the largest killers of our time. We orchestrated ourselves out of a strong treaty to create an international criminal tribunal. We are the stingiest aid donor of all of the major countries of the world. And the one creative act in foreign policy that we have accomplished in the last six or seven years, the enlargement of NATO, is really a step backwards rather than a step forward, because it's primarily an effort to restore American domination in Europe at the cost of a relationship with Russia.

Moreover, our constitutional system seems to be deteriorating. Congress is micromanaging almost every foreign policy issue: every member of Congress thinks of himself or herself as a Secretary of State. So sensible resolutions to such problems as trade negotiation, an approach to Cuba, the right to abortion, and our responsibility to pay our dues to the UN have all been frustrated by the Congress. In short, I end gloomily, it may be time to conclude that like the Greek Republic, the Roman Empire, Napoleon's France and the British Empire, the United States has had its day. We are still a great power, especially in an economic sense, but we seem to be a great power in decline.

Dwayne A. Gathers '80. I would add to what Ambassador Zimmermann has said by going back to my senior year at Deerfield in 1980 and two courses that I took simultaneously, one taught by Russ Miller entitled "What

Went Wrong?" which explored the period after World War II through the Cold War and the break-up of the world into two power blocs, the Soviet Union and the United States, and another course taught by Jay Morsman entitled "Power of the Presidency." Remembering those two courses from the position I am in now, stationed in Johannesburg, South Africa, we can look at the issue of what went wrong and what is going right, if anything, particularly during the period after the fall of the Berlin Wall.

From my little piece of the world, roughly 8,000 miles away from here, we continue to see the promise of a new world order deteriorate into tensions fueled in large part by issues of race, ethnicity and the like. But I think the challenge in 1998, compared to when I left here in 1980, really is the medium by which we now have access to what is going on. Back in the Cold War days you had a bunch of men sitting in rooms negotiating deals, which in effect excluded substantial parts of the world. We now call those parts "emerging markets." Now we have many more players on the scene who have access to things such as the Internet and CNN. There is no greater equalizer to international news and the dissemination of information than CNN. In the 1940s and 1950s there wasn't a CNN to disseminate what was going on in the world. The challenge now is the question: does the West have a fatigue factor with all of these dangers, whether they be Southeast Asia or Africa or the Middle East? And does the American presidency really have the capacity to effect a strong leadership role over a dictator who controls oil in Angola?

In my time at the State Department back in 1991-92, my boss, then-Ambassador Herman Cohen, the Assistant Secretary for African Affairs, conducted a seminar for African ambassadors in Washington. As we were riding over to Georgetown, he said to me, "What do you think of this question? Who controls foreign policy in the United States? Is it the president? Does a member of the third district of Mississippi have more power in U.S. foreign policy? Is it the media? Is it corporate America? Is it the activist/lobbyist groups?"

Barton. How do you develop the argument that something terrible that is happening in a particular place is worthy of the human sacrifice, the financial sacrifice and the leadership sacrifice the U.S. would need to take to intervene?

Zimmermann. I do think if there is genocide anywhere in the world, there have to be ways to deal with it. The logical way is through a multi-lateral system, the U.N. The U.S. is now in a period where we should be involved in a transition from being the great power, where we lead on almost every-thing, to being a country which helps to lead within organizations like NATO and particularly the U.N. But you look around and you discover we are about lose our vote in the U.N. General Assembly because we haven't paid our dues. The ability to respond to a human catastrophe is going to be cast aside because we're not prepared to make the U.N. an organization that can respond to these kinds of challenges.

I think one of the challenges, as I said before, is the simple deter-mination of what is in our interest. Clearly we as the leading nation in the world, one imbued with so many gifts, have always felt that we have a chal-lenge to lead and be a force for good. If I go back to our ninth grade required course, "Shaping Western Society," and look at the contents of that course versus where we are now, good chunks of the world simply were left out of "SWS." The point is, if you're sitting in suburban Los Angeles and you're inundated with televised scenes of horror and you have no educational or pro-fessional basis for understanding where that country is on the map, much less why that country might matter, then the president has a problem mobiliz-ing American interest in that concern.

I think we should look at the present period as a transition toward a time when the United States is sacrificing a good deal of its dominance in foreign policy to international organizations and thinking in cooperative terms. We're not thinking in terms like that. Our Congress is talking as if we were the only country with any power in the world. I think the whole mindset has got to be changed. Just as in the Cold War we were looked to as a leader, now we have to be prepared to see some of that leadership devolve upon other countries and upon organizations in which we would play an important role but not necessarily a dominant one.

[in response to an audience question about Kosovo] Kosovo is a very tough situation, as I think everybody knows. Military force by itself isn't going to be enough because there has to be some kind of vision of what kind of constitutional situation you want. This is a typical post-Cold War situa-tion in which no one country, certainly not the United States, can do every-thing by itself. We are going somehow to have to impose a constitutional res-olution on the issue, and that's very hard to do.

Barton. I think the issue of "followership" is another part of leadership, and there are some people who work with the world community who find it every bit as fragmented and difficult to pull together as they feel critical of the United States for its inability to seize that role. I remember talking to the head of the United Nations High Commission for Refugees of the former

Yugoslavia, and she said, "If you believe that the Europeans can work in unison, let me just say the following words—mad cow disease."

Gathers. When we talk about U.S. leadership, it has been assumed and expected on the part of many in the world community that South Africa would take the lead with regard to African problems. Part of the challenge we have with that is that some of those friends who were acknowledged quite publicly by Nelson Mandela tend to be people who are abhorred by the United States: Fidel Castro, Muammar Kaddafi of Libya, and Hassad of Syria. Mandela is unapologetic when he says, "These are people who stood with us," for fundamentally he believes the U.S. did not stand with them and fight against apartheid. When you've been fighting your own battles for 50 years and you just now are becoming a governmental entity, you simply don't have time to be the heavy force that some would want you to be.

Barton. Our second panel is looking at the environment we live in, and our two panelists are Gil Grosvenor, who gave us at breakfast this morning the secret formula for improving his grade in chemistry from C to A in his senior year (pitching for Mr. Boyden's baseball team while Mrs. Boyden was the score-keeper), and Kerry Emanuel, who was the president of the Weather Club when he was here.

Gilbert M. Grosvenor '49. Simply put, the future quality of life on earth will depend upon our ability to live within sustainable consumption and sustainable development of our natural resources. Before we even dream of such accomplishments, I think several things have to happen. Globally we must achieve population stability, at home we must develop a skilled cadre of sensitive environmentalists, and we must produce a cadre of teachers to educate every American citizen. Education is absolutely crucial to understanding global/environmental issues. We must produce a generation of politicians and diplomats who have extraordinary and sensitive negotiating skills.

For example, let's hypothetically suppose that China decides to utilize its huge resources of high sulfur coal, and build hundreds of coal-fired generator plants in China to jump-start its economy. This would be absolutely disastrous to our atmosphere; it would destroy the ozone layer. How could the international community approach China and somehow convince them that this is a very bad idea? Another example, a reality issue: Eastern European nations are laced with pre-Chernobyl reactors; meltdown is inevitable; it's just a matter of when. Of course the Nordic countries will take the brunt of it, but the entire planet will suffer immense damage if one of those reactors really melts down to a serious state. How are we, as a part of the international community, going to help solve that problem? Clearly Eastern Europe can't afford to abandon those reactors and build new ones. We will somehow, as an international community, have to find a way to deal with that problem.

But I think the biggest problem is population stability. Exponential growth has been developing over the last century and is now the most serious problem facing the twenty-first century. Let me put it into a little perspective. In the year 1650 there were half a billion people on planet Earth; we were doubling in 250 years. By 1900 that doubling was down to 70 years and by 1971 we were doubling in 20 years. In 1991 we had almost 6 billion people on the planet, and while the doubling rate has slowed some, it's still impossible to sustain that kind of growth. The question is, can we as an international community slow that down? Otherwise nature will take its course: war, hunger, starvation, thirst, disease will control the population.

We also have to consider the tremendous stress that we've put on our natural resources. Ultimately the world's finite supply of renewable resources will diminish to the point where our quality of life will be endangered. Clearly, in my mind anyway, water will be the first signal. Water is an issue now in 26 countries, a tenth of the countries in the world. Our oceans, 97 percent of our water, are clearly at risk. Only international cooperation can really revive the great harvests of the ocean.

And don't think the U.S. doesn't have environmental challenges. Our population in the twentieth century has shifted dramatically. We've gone from a rural population to an urban one. Since 1900 the population in the United States has tripled, yet during this century 85 percent of our counties have lost population. We have become a nation of city-dwellers. Contributing to this shift, of course, is the emergence of the automobile, which has given us mobility. It's given us independence, it's changed our social patterns, and it has also dramatically polluted our atmosphere and changed our landscape. If you put all the paved roads in the United States together, they would cover all of the New England states.

Kerry A. Emanuel '73. I'd like to talk a little bit about approaches that might be taken to solving some of these problems. The approaches are going to be very different from those we've taken in the past. When I was a student here at Deerfield in the early 1970s, science was going through the dawning throes of a very long and productive era that concentrated in what we call "reductionist science." There is an aesthetic behind this, which I very much subscribed to at the time. This was simply to try to understand the natural world and to attack each of the problems as a microcosm. The ultimate goal of reductionism, as its name implies, is to describe the entire world in a very simple compact set. In the realm of physics, the goal for a long time has been unified field theory, where a few equations describe everything, essentially, that's going on in the universe. So strong was this aesthetic that it spilled over into realms which previously had been considered to lie outside of science. So we have such things as political science, which to an educated person of the 19th century, would have been regarded as a terrible oxymoron. Reductionist science had its roots in the Enlightenment, and elements of reductionism can certainly be found in the Greek philosophers.

What the world has not quite come to terms with yet is that a lot of the problems we face, the kind that Gil described particularly, don't lend themselves to a reductionist approach. If you wanted to pin the entire transition down to one incident, you could say that the seeds of the end of reductionism were sown in 1962, when a colleague of mine at MIT was trying to run one of the first numerical weather predictions on a very old computer whose vacuum tubes were constantly blowing out and having to be replaced, and so he decided to restart a calculation he was doing in weather forecasts. He went out to get a cup of coffee, and he came back expecting to see that the computer simulation had proceeded exactly the same way the last one had, since he'd started with the same numbers, only to find that he was looking at completely different numbers. He said, "Oh well, one of the vacuum tubes is blown," and tried to get some of the technicians to look at it, but in fact the computer was fine. That was arguably the birth of the notion of chaos, which we are now familiar with; it's the idea that probably most of the systems of interest to us are inherently not predictable. And it also introduced the notion of complexity.

I think it will be very difficult for the young people in the audience to understand, as recently as 20 years ago, the terrific resistance that the scientific community had to the notion of complexity in chaos. I remember taking a class from a famous man, Edward Lorenz, in the 1960s, where he described the so-called "butterfly effect," where a butterfly, flapping its wings outside somewhere could entirely change the course of the world's weather if you waited long enough. Nobody believed it; the senior physics professors at MIT certainly didn't believe it at the time. Now we have come to take it for granted. What does this all mean for us?

Global warming is probably the preeminent example of a nonreductionist problem in science. For years we've looked for the holy grail of global warming: there must be some trick where we could understand how to predict how the climate would evolve in response to greenhouse gases.

Apparently such a trick doesn't exist. It is an enormously complex system; the uncertainties associated with making a prediction are so large as to render predictions, at this time, almost useless. How do we as a society operate when that's the nature of the problem?

It requires a very different aesthetic for how to do science and how to solve problems. There is always the notion, perpetrated by Hollywood, of the mad scientist working away in a dark laboratory in the top of a tower, and in fact, to some approximation, some scientists did work that way, in a solitary mode, and they solved very important problems. Very few of the remaining important problems, I think, can be solved by that approach because we've moved into a realm where no single person on earth has the expertise to solve these pressing problems; people have to work in teams. This, I think, is something we're just learning how to do. For global warming there isn't one person who knows enough about just the atmosphere, let alone the ocean, the earth, the biosphere, to solve the important problems. Then as we spill into the political sphere, how do we make policy decisions in this framework of uncertainty? That's a new ballgame for the human race. And it's going to be up to you to decide how to play that.

Barton. One thing we've found in the Nobel Peace Prize, which was awarded last year to the land mine activists, was that the Nobel Committee was trying to recognize organizing groups beyond governments and international bodies; citizen groups that can get together and address an important issue and get out ahead of their government structures, which is again a model that I think everybody's looking for, as suggested in some of these comments.

Grosvenor (answering an audience question about education). The one attribute that you see in all population statistics is education. Those countries that have the best educated populations generally have realistic, controllable populations; there is a correlation between education and population stability. As for global environmental issues, it's very difficult for an individual citizen to impact a global issue, but it is the best way to impact domestic issues. For example, the Nashua River in New Hampshire was so polluted that people would take bets on what color it would run from one day to the next. For twenty years you were risking your life to get near that river. One woman, Mary Stoddard, spent twenty years, but she cleaned that river up, basically by herself. Individuals are crucial at the local area. On a global issue I think you have to go to organizations and governments.

Barton. Kerry, you've suggested a model where the scientists are not working in solitary, but they're really getting together and addressing these problems as a community—do you have any examples that you can share?

Emanuel. Certainly. I'll go back to the example of global warming, something that concerns me with respect to education. That is, we have to start to teach people how to work together on problems as teams. The global warming problem, if it's going to be solved, is going to be solved by people who understand how to come together and to share ideas and expertise. Of course there is still a pressing need to educate people into narrow, highly advanced pieces of expertise. You simply have to have that, but how do you bring these people together? How do you get them talking to each other? Some amazing breakthroughs have occurred in the global warming problem in recent years simply by getting oceanographers and biologists to talk to one another.

Barton. Our third section is going to address the financial world. Obviously our economic system has been heralded as improving the prospects for the world community. The leaders for this panel are Carrie Freeman and Dozier Gardner.

M. Dozier Gardner '51. I'll sketch out a little descriptive information about what's been happening in the world's capital markets, and in particular the United States, and then Carrie will talk about it a little more personally and what it's meant in terms of her career path. I think all of us are aware that the world and particularly the United States has been in an extraordinary, with few exceptions, economic boom. In this country alone, we've had seven years of prosperity without a single quarter of down economic activity. It has increased employment, it has produced exceptional investment returns, the corporate profitability is very high, and I think that, notwithstanding the pessimistic comments that Warren has expressed, this has had important spill-over effects on the rest of the world.

Some of the pretty straightforward causes have been important new technologies in communications and information processing, opening of previously controlled or sheltered markets of enterprise, deregulation and privatization, reduction in military expenditures—pretty much around the world —declining inflation, and the ready availability of low-cost capital. I think that's what's behind this boom. Some of the implications are, of course, that there's been exceptional wealth creation in this country and abroad too. Two little measures of that: in the last two decades the U.S. stock market's returns have averaged something like 18 percent per year. And bond market returns have been very high. A company like Microsoft, which was started by a college dropout, went public in 1986, and now the value of all its shareholders' ownings is close to 300 billion dollars, which is about the size of the entire Brazilian stock market. It is four times the size of General Motors.

If you look at compensation in various industries around the United States, you see every day some of the effects of this boom. Another effect is that it's caused a very important shift in the preference of investors towards common stocks; a decade ago 14 percent of U.S. households owned some common stocks; today 35 percent do. Stocks are generally the preference in retirement plans. Another clear implication, or fallout, is the development of wonderful industries. I talked about Microsoft, but there have been the same kind of revolutionary changes in the biotechnology industry, communications, the Internet; even in education there have been some very interesting and important privately financed efforts to revolutionize secondary education.

I think one pretty obvious question now is, are we riding for a fall? All kinds of good things build in bad behavior, and we're seeing some of the results in bankruptcies, bad lending practices, improper investment activity. I think a much more difficult question is whether this free-enterprise, open-global-markets framework is the right framework for a developing world. Only perhaps 40 percent of countries and 20 percent of the population are enjoying the benefit of this kind of boom. Twenty percent of the population in the richest countries consume 80 percent of the world's goods and services. So there's an exceptionally uneven distribution of wealth, even though there has been tremendous wealth creation.

Carrie E. Freeman '92. I graduated from Dartmouth College in '96, and when I showed up for my first day of work, I entered a class of about 140 analysts in my same position, and about half of us were going to stay in the United States, dispersed throughout the country, and then the other half were going to go abroad, dispersed around the world. I think that that was my initial understanding of how global the business world is, just by, after a month of training, having friends in places I had never visited, which may have been a purpose of the training at the same time. I think that my analyst class was just a reflection of how global business has become, and how much the need has shifted toward figuring out an international strategy.

When I was at Goldman Sachs the clients demanded global coverage, and now at Disney I find that there's a consumer demand for localized Disney content. With that comes the responsibility to understand on the one hand your clients on the banking or consulting side, but then also on the distribution side you have to understand the market that you're trying to deliver to: tastes, things like that. It's the coordination, I find, (especially at the junior level) that takes up a lot of time. In the morning I'm speaking with people in Europe and Paris and London and then have to wait until late afternoon to call people in Asia. A part of my daily life at work is straddling time zones; I find that to be pretty challenging.

To tie it back to Deerfield, I turned back to the trusty Deerfield catalogue, which opens with the mission statement, "to wrestle with ideas, to see another's point of view, to discover something about how the world works, to live with others of different backgrounds, beliefs, or interests." That to me is central to how I set out into the workplace. To some extent my education has just continued after school, and sometimes I'm surprised I get paid for it; sometimes I feel I'm learning more than I'm adding. The skills that you develop at Deerfield in terms of how to approach a problem, how to have an open discussion, how to research, how to execute as an individual or on a team, are all skills which prepare you very well for not only the workplace but life. No matter what you end up doing in terms of a job, you have to keep in mind that it's always a learning process.

Gardner. Harvard biologist Edward Wilson wrote that the proven formulas for prosperity are being eagerly adopted by the rest of the world, and he says that even if the industrialization of the developing countries is only partly successful, the environmental after-shock will dwarf the population explosion that preceded it.

Gathers. Some of that exporting of American values is in part played by American corporations. While some in France might rue the "Disneyfication" of Europe and the world, certainly American companies have in many instances brought in systems, management, technologies, and ways of doing business and of being a corporate citizen, that have raised the level of discourse and raised the level of awareness of environmental issues and employee management issues in developing countries. Clearly there's a long way to go. If you're a village in Nigeria, you say, we have oil; we don't worry too much about the whole environmental issue; we worry about eating tonight. But to the extent that there's a U.S. company involved in that oil extraction process, there's the ability at least to bring some of our Western ideas to addressing these global issues.

Freeman. It's difficult to talk about having a global culture, because to some extent, and I've seen it at Disney, you have to localize Mickey Mouse, for example. It doesn't work to have the same content, the same education, the same values in every different market, in every different country, in every different town or village. I wonder what the balance is between exporting a value system and also in localizing.

Barton. Isolation for the United States is not an option—it's not possible, for many of the reasons you've heard today: the extraordinary interconnection of the financial and economic world, the connection of the big problems like the environment, global warming, population and so forth. The question is not whether we will be isolated; the question is what sort of engagement in the world we choose.

Gathers. It's a more complex world. As we went through school, we were always told that the U.S. was the preeminent power in the world based on the foundation of the Constitution, and we did believe that. In 1998 there are a lot more players with a lot more means at their disposal to neutralize some of that power. One thing we really haven't touched on is the role of technology today, in terms of global capital markets, in terms of global information, in terms of how messages are played across the world from a geopolitical standpoint, the use of media and the Internet.

Barton. I know I said at the beginning of our panel discussion that sometimes the best kind of leadership is "followership": the ten people who will follow somebody who has a grain of an idea. We also have to look for broader-gauged thinking: no matter how much of a specialist you are and however well you're doing in your chosen profession, you do have to engage and connect to other careers and areas of interest as well. Those are some of the themes that I think were mentioned today.

OUR CONTRIBUTORS AND THEIR CONTRIBUTIONS

Frederick D. Barton '67 is the Director of the U.S. Agency for International Development (USAID) Office of Transition Initiatives. A talk, "Taking Deerfield to the Ends of the Earth," April, 1997, and remarks as Moderator of the panel discussion, "Through a Looking Glass Brightly," October, 1998.

Robert B. Binswanger '48P has spent one half of his 45 years as an educator in the private sector and one half in the public sector. He has served most recently as a member of the Department of Defense Overseas Schools and the Harvard University Visiting Committee. Remarks in the panel discussion, "A Moving Picture," October, 1998.

Thomas D. Bloomer '49P has retired from his position as Personnel Manager at IBM. Remarks in the panel discussion, "The Future is Upon Us," November, 1997.

Steven D. Brill '68P, founder of *The American Lawyer* magazine and Courtroom Television Network, is Chairman of Brill Media Ventures and Editor-in-Chief of *Brill's Content*. Remarks in the panel discussion, "A Moving Picture," October, 1998.

Peter M. Buchanan '53 is retired President of the Council for Advancement and Support of Education (CASE). Remarks in the panel discussion, "The Future is Upon Us," November, 1997.

Former President George H. W. Bush was President of the United States, 1989-1993. He served previously as Vice President of the United States, 1981-1989, and as U.S. Ambassador to the United Nations, head of the U.S. Liaison Office in Beijing, Director of Central Intelligence, and member of the U.S. House of Representatives. Commencement speech, "Some Advice from an Optimist," June, 1997.

Senator John H. Chafee '40P has served as Senator from Rhode Island since 1976. He was Secretary of the Navy, 1969-1972 and Governor of Rhode Island, 1962-1969. Convocation speech, "Never Give In," September, 1997.

Thomas G. Clark '67P is a Deerfield apple farmer. Remarks in the panel discussion, "Refracting the Past," October, 1998.

Elizabeth M. Clement S'66 is Minister for Church Life and Education at the First Congregational Church, UCC, in Atlanta, Georgia. Remarks in the panel discussion, "A Moving Picture," and the sermon, "The Gifts of Memory," October, 1998.

Eliot R. Cutler '64P is a partner in the Washington, DC and Denver law firm of

Cutler and Stanfield, which specializes in environmental land use law. Remarks in the panel discussion, "A Moving Picture," October, 1998.

Charles E. Danielski '53 is a teacher of Mathematics, Biology and Geology at Deerfield Academy. Remarks in the panel discussion, "Refracting the Past," October, 1998.

Paul Didisheim, M.D. '45 is Head of the Biomaterials Program in the Division of Heart and Vascular Disease at the National Heart, Lung and Blood Institute of the National Institutes of Health in Bethesda, Maryland. Remarks in the panel discussion, "Medical Practice: What's New, What's Not," September, 1997.

Kerry A. Emanuel '73 is Professor in the Program in Atmospheres, Oceans and Climate, Department of Earth, Atmospheric and Planetary Sciences, at M.I.T. Remarks in the panel discussion, "Through a Looking Glass Brightly," October, 1998.

Erik C. Esselstyn '55 is Founder and President of Cross Creek Initiatives, an environmental protection organization, and is working on assembling a fleet of hydrogen fuel cell vehicles on the University of Florida campus. Remarks in the panel discussion, "The Future is Upon Us," November, 1997.

Suzanne L. Flynt is the Curator of the Memorial Hall Museum of the Pocumtuck Valley Memorial Association in Deerfield. A talk to students, "Life at Deerfield Academy 200 Years Ago," January, 1999.

Carrie E. Freeman '92 is Analyst in Strategic Planning at the Walt Disney Company. Remarks in the panel discussion, "Through a Looking Glass Brightly," October, 1998.

Donald R. Friary P'92,'93 is Executive Director and Secretary, Historic Deerfield, Inc. Remarks in the panel discussion, "Refracting the Past," October, 1998.

M. Dozier Gardner '51 is Vice Chairman and a Director of Eaton Vance Corporation. Remarks in the panel discussion, "Through a Looking Glass Brightly," October, 1998.

Dwayne A. Gathers '80 is the first Director of the State of California's Office of Trade and Investment in Johannesburg, South Africa. Remarks in the panel discussion, "Through a Looking Glass Brightly," October, 1998.

Gilbert M. Grosvenor '49 is Chairman of the National Geographic Society's Board of Trustees and Educational Foundation. Remarks in the panel discussion, "Through a Looking Glass Brightly," October, 1998.

Samuel A. Hartwell '48 is CEO of the G.S. Blodgett Corporation and Chairman of STRIVE, the East Harlem employment service. Remarks in the panel discussion, "The Future is Upon Us," November, 1997.

Karinne T. Heise is Chair of the English Department at Deerfield Academy. Remarks in the panel discussion, "Refracting the Past," October, 1998.

Thomas A. Heise is Chair of the History Department at Deerfield Academy. Remarks in the panel discussion, "Refracting the Past," October, 1998; "A Deerfield Welcome" to new students, September, 1998; and a talk, "As Natural as Breathing," June, 1998.

Frank C. Henry Jr. '69 is former Chair of the English Department at Deerfield Academy and Clerk to the Board of Trustees. He is on sabbatical for the year 1999-2000. A talk "Keeping the Watch," in the panel discussion, "Our School at the Millennium," October, 1998.

Wanda S. Henry is former Chair of the Mathematics Department at Deerfield Academy. She is on sabbatical for the year 1999-2000. Excerpts from her presentation on Mrs. Boyden, on behalf of the Mathematics Department, September, 1997.

Alice S. Ilchman P'85 is Chairman of the Board of Trustees of the Rockefeller Foundation and President Emerita of Sarah Lawrence College. "Deerfield at 200," The Bicentennial Address.

Warren F. Ilchman P'85 is Director of the Paul and Daisy Soros Fellowships for New Americans and Executive Director Emeritus of the Indiana University Center on Philanthropy. "Deerfield at 200," The Bicentennial Address.

Patricia McNerney Kelleher '48 is Vice Principal for Academic Affairs at the Bishop Feehan High School in Attleboro, Massachusetts. Remarks in the panel discussion, "The Future is Upon Us," November, 1997.

Kendrick P. Lance, M.D. '45 is a physician retired from his practice, Gastrointestinal Associates, in New Jersey. Remarks as Moderator of the panel, "Medical Practice: What's New, What's Not," September, 1997.

Edwin P. Maynard, M.D. '44 is a practicing physician and teacher in the Massachusetts General Hospital and Harvard Medical School system, with an interest in the delivery of health care and in health care issues. Remarks in the panel discussion, "Medical Practice: What's New, What's Not," September, 1997.

Robert E. McCabe Jr., M.D. '44 has retired from his work as a transplant surgeon at Columbia Presbyterian Medical School and St. Luke's Hospital in New York City. Remarks in the panel discussion, "Medical Practice: What's New, What's Not," September, 1997.

Ferrell P. McClean P'94, '98 is Managing Director for J.P. Morgan's global investment banking business with the energy, mining and power industries. Remarks in the panel discussion, "A Moving Picture," October, 1998.

Malcolm McKenzie, Principal emeritus of the Maru a Pula School, Gaborone, Botswana, is the Deerfield Bicentennial Scholar, 1999-2000 and the headmaster-elect of Atlantic College, Wales.

John A. Mendelson '58 founded and runs Champlain Asset Management and is Chief Market Analyst for Charles Schwab Company. Remarks in the panel discussion, "The Future is Upon Us," November, 1997.

Robert L. Merriam '43P, Faculty Emeritus, is a used, rare, and antique book dealer in Conway, Massachusetts. A talk, "Schoolmastering," in the panel discussion, "Our School at the Millennium," October, 1998.

John C. O'Brien P'87, '91, '92 is a teacher of English at Deerfield Academy. A talk on behalf of the English Department, "The Child is Father of the Man," April, 1997.

Brian A. Rosborough '58P is Founder and Chairman of the Earthwatch Institute. Remarks as Moderator on two panels, "The Future is Upon Us," November, 1997, and "Refracting the Past," October, 1998; and a talk, "Back to the Future," June, 1997.

Stephen G. Smith '67P is Editor of *U.S. News and World Report*. Remarks as Moderator of the panel, "A Moving Picture," October, 1998.

Meera S. Viswanathan H'95 is Associate Professor of Comparative Literature and East Asian Studies, Brown University, and teacher of English and History, Deerfield Academy. Remarks in closing the homecoming program for the Classes of 1948-1959, "Homeward Bound," November, 1997.

Porter K. Wheeler '58P is Transportation Policy and Financial Consultant for Apogee Research, Bethesda, Maryland. Remarks in the panel discussion, "The Future is Upon Us," November, 1997.

Warren Zimmermann '52, US Ambassador to Yugoslavia, 1989-1992, is the Kathryn and Shelby Cullom Davis Professor in the Practice of International Diplomacy at Columbia University. Remarks in the panel discussion, "Through a Looking Glass Brightly," October, 1998.

BICENTENNIAL PROGRAMS

On the next few pages we list speeches, symposia and presentations that
occurred during the six homecoming weekends and the Grand Celebration.
These were produced directly from programs of the events;
some contributors' roles or work have changed since the time of their participation.

HOMECOMING SYMPOSIA — APRIL 1997 —- CLASSES OF 1960-68

Thursday, April 17
DEERFIELD AT 200

> Moderator: *Peter G. Hindle '52, Teacher of Mathematics*
> Panelists: *Martha C. Lyman, Assistant Headmaster, Director of College Advising*
> *Richard A. Bonanno P'91, Dean of the Faculty*
> *D. Gordon MacLeod P'93,'95,'99, Academic Dean*
> *Patricia L. Gimbel P'87, Dean of Admission and Financial Aid*

Friday, April 18
LIFE AFTER DEERFIELD ACADEMY

> Why the Public Hates the Press
> *Henry P. Becton Jr. '61, President, WGBH Educational Foundation*
> *Steven D. Brill '68, CEO of American Lawyer Media and Founder of Court TV*
> *Stephen G. Smith '67P, Editor, National Journal*

A CELEBRATION OF THE PERFORMING ARTS: 1797-1997

> Premiere of *Deerfield Always We Remember,* an original composition by G. Gregory
> Bullen with text by Andrea Moorhead
> Deerfield Academy Chorus and Instrumentalists

Saturday, April 19
THE WORLD BEYOND HUCK FINN AND DAVID COPPERFIELD, English Department

> Introduction: *Frank C. Henry Jr., '69, Chair, English Department*
>
> The Teacher is Father to the Child
> *Arthur J. Clement '66, Trustee, Deerfield Academy and*
> *President, Clement & Wynn Program Managers*
>
> English Department Classes
>
> "The Child is the Father of the Man"
> *John C. O'Brien P'87, '91, '92, Teacher of English, College Advisor*
>
> Taking Deerfield to the Ends of the Earth
> *Frederick D. Barton '67, Director, US AID*
> *Bureau for Humanitarian Response, Office of Transition Initiatives*
>
> Closing Remarks and Farewell
> *Meera S. Viswanathan H'95, Teacher of History and English*
> *Eric Widmer '57, Headmaster, Teacher of History*

HOMECOMING SYMPOSIA — JUNE 1997 — CLASSES OF 1981-89

Friday, June 12
WHAT HAS CHANGED AT DEERFIELD SINCE THE 80S?

Moderator: *Peter G. Hindle '52, Teacher of Mathematics*
Panelists: *Elizabeth A. McNamara, Assistant Dean of the Faculty, Teacher of English*
Richard A. Bonanno P'91, Dean of the Faculty
G. Alan Fraker P'88, '95, '98, Chair, History Department
Patricia L. Gimbel P'87, Dean of Admission and Financial Aid

LIFE AFTER DEERFIELD: ALUMNI OF THE 80S

Moderator: *Michael S. Cary P'02, Headmaster, The Lawrenceville School*
Panelists: *Peter F. Nelson '81, Author and tree house builder*
Nelson A. Rockefeller Jr. '82, Former Policy Assistant to Senator Bob Dole,
Co-Manager – South Texas Ranch
Christopher J. Waddell '87, Paralympic Gold Medalist,
Model for The Shot Modeling Agency in NYC
Craig H. Janney '85, Member, Phoenix Coyotes Hockey Team
Joseph S. Caldwell IV '81, Private art dealer, The Caldwell Gallery

Saturday, June 14
SENSE OF PLACE, Science Department

Welcome *Andrew B. Harcourt P'97, '02, Chair, Science Department*

"And Know the Place for the First Time"
David C. Howell '65P, Teacher of Science, Planetarium Director

Hands on experience with new technology
Student Assistants: *Sarah Bowman '98, James Colbert '98, Jonathan Rohrs '97*
Samantha Sacks '97, Joshua Platt '00, Starvonsky Gibbs-Phillip '99,
Phillip Chin '98, Paul Nicholson '98

"Back to the Future"
Brian A. Rosborough '58P, Trustee, Deerfield Academy and President, CEO Earthwatch
Expeditions

Closing Remarks
Meera S. Viswanathan H'95, Associate Professor of Comparative Literature, Brown
University
Teacher of English and History
Eric Widmer '57, Headmaster; Teacher of History

HOMECOMING SYMPOSIA — SEPTEMBER 1997 — CLASSES OF 1912-47

Friday, September 12
DEERFIELD AT 200

>Moderator: *Peter G. Hindle '52, Teacher of Mathematics*
>Panelists: *Martha C. Lyman, Assistant Headmaster, Director of College Advising*
>*Richard A. Bonanno P'91, Dean of the Faculty*
>*D. Gordon MacLeod P'93,'95,'99, Academic Dean*
>*Patricia L. Gimbel P'87, Dean of Admission and Financial Aid*

ARCHIVAL EXHIBITS, EXHIBITION BY DEERFIELD ART TEACHERS

LIFE AFTER DEERFIELD

>Medical Practice: What's New, What's Not
>Moderator: *Kendrick P. Lance, M.D. '45, Physician (Retired),*
>*Gastrointestinal Associates, NJ*
>Panelists: *Edwin P. Maynard, M.D. '44, Physician/Teacher, Massachusetts*
>*General Hospital/Harvard University*
>*Paul Didisheim, M.D. '45, Head, Biomaterials Program, Division of Heart and*
>*Vascular Disease, NHLBI, Bethesda, MD*
>*Robert E. McCabe Jr., M.D. '44, Surgeon (Retired), St. Luke's Hospital, NYC*

BICENTENNIAL CONVOCATION

>Keynote Address: *The Hon. John H. Chafee '40, U.S. Senator, Rhode Island*

Saturday, September 13
REMEMBERING HELEN CHILDS BOYDEN, Mathematics Department

>Slide Presentation of Mrs. Boyden in Her Many Roles
>
>The Words of Mrs. Boyden
>*Wanda S. Henry, Chair of Mathematics Department*
>
>Letters to Mrs. Boyden
>*Leander E. Magee, Teacher of Mathematics*
>
>Panel: Anecdotes and Conversation about Mrs. Boyden
>Panel Leader: *Peter G. Hindle '52, Teacher of Mathematics*
>Panelists: *Roland W. Young P'88, Teacher of Mathematics*
>*Ruth and Laurence E. Bohrer P'77, Teacher and Chair of Science Dept. (Ret.)*
>*Linus Travers '54, Professor of English, University of Massachusetts*
>*Member of Board of Trustees, Emeritus*
>*John H. Suitor '34PG, Teacher of English (Ret.)*
>*Robert L. Merriam '43P, Teacher of English (Ret.)*

DEERFIELD MATHEMATICS: FROM THE SLIDE RULE TO THE HAND-HELD COMPUTER

Demonstration by Mathematics Faculty:
Robert P. Hammond P'93,'94
Henrianne V. Hammond P'93,'94
John F. Graney P'81,'83
D. Gordon MacLeod P'93,'95,'99
Pamela A. Bonanno P'91
Conclusion: *Wanda S. Henry*

Technology Display
Faculty: *Sheryl A. Cabral*
Marc J. Dancer '79
Sean D. Keller '86
Sidney S. Smith
Tara J. Slesar
Matthew J. Lisa
Students: *Spencer Cherry '98*
Kate Forssell '98
Joel Panock '98
Paul Nicholson '98
Mathew Rogers '98
Casey Driskill '00
Josh Platt '00

Technology Projects
Student Demonstration:
Marc Cartright '98
George Pence '98
Mark Kidd '98
Chad Steinglass '98
Julian Wassenaar '98
Tamara Brisk '99

Multi-Media Display:
Edward V. Hammond '93, MIT '97

CLOSING REMARKS
Meera S. Viswanathan H'95, Associate Professor of Comparative Literature, Brown University
Teacher of History and English, Deerfield Academy

Homecoming Symposia — November 1997 — Classes of 1948-59

Friday, November 7
Deerfield at 200

>Moderator: *Robert M. Dewey Jr. '49, President, Deerfield Board of Trustees*
>Panelists: *Eric Widmer '57, Headmaster*
>*Meera S. Viswanathan H'95, Associate Professor of Comparative Literature, Brown University*
>*Teacher of English and History, Deerfield Academy*
>*Patricia L. Gimbel P'87, Dean of Admission and Financial Aid*
>*D. Gordon MacLeod P'93,'95,'99, Academic Dean*

Archival Exhibits: American Paintings from the Charles P. Russell Collection

Life after Deerfield

>The Future is Upon Us: Forecasts from the Field
>Moderator: *Brian A. Rosborough '58P, President, CEO Earthwatch Expeditions*
>Panelists: *Patricia M. Kelleher '48, Vice Principal for Academic Affairs,*
>*Bishop Feehan High School*
>*Samuel A. Hartwell '48, CEO, G.S. Blodgett Corporation; Chairman of STRIVE*
>*Thomas D. Bloomer '49, Personnel Manager (ret.), IBM*
>*Peter M. Buchanan '53, President (ret.), CASE*
>*Erik C. Esselstyn '55, President, Cross Creek Initiatives*
>*John A. Mendelson '58, Chief Market Analyst, Charles Schwab Co., NYC*
>*Porter K. Wheeler '58, Transportation Policy and Financial Consultant, Apogee Research*

Saturday, November 8
Linking Deerfield Academy to the World, Language Department

>Introduction: *Eric Widmer '57, Headmaster*
>*Claudia Lyons, Language Department Chair*

>Let's talk! Parlons! Sprechen wir! Hablemos! Discamus!

>The Role of Deerfield in Our Lives and in Our Outlooks
>Introduction: *Eric Widmer '57*
>Presenters: *Ann Kerr, wife of Malcolm Kerr '49,*
>*President of American University, Beirut 1982-84*
>*John Waterbury '57, President Elect, American University,Beirut*

Closing Remarks

>*Meera S. Viswanathan H'95, Associate Professor of Comparative Literature, Brown University*
>*Teacher of History and English, Deerfield Academy*

HOMECOMING SYMPOSIA — APRIL 1998 — CLASSES OF 1969-80

Saturday, April 25
THE MAKING OF A TRADITION: ARTISTIC EXPRESSION AT DEERFIELD ACADEMY
Fine Arts Department

>Introduction: *John H. Reese P'88, Chair, Fine Arts Department*
>Moderator: *Daniel Hodermarsky, Former Faculty*
>Panelists: *Sara Bowman '98*
>*Chris Burns '86*
>*George Knight '85*
>*Tom Locke '92*
>*Will Ouimet '97*
>*Christina Rosenberger '98*
>*Matt Scannell '88*
>*Martin Sweeney '86*
>*Max Williams '92*

>Tours of Fine Arts Facilities — *Led by Deerfield Students*

ARCHIVAL EXHIBITS, ALUMNI SHOW

LIFE AFTER DEERFIELD — ALUMNI SYMPOSIUM
>Moderator: *Josh Binswanger '80*
>Panelists: *Fred Bendheim '74*
>*Stephen Hannock '70*
>*Accra Shepp '80*
>*Sam Weisman '65*
>*Jim Wilson '74*

A CELEBRATION OF THE PERFORMING ARTS: 1797-1997

HOMECOMING SYMPOSIUM — JUNE 1998 — CLASSES OF 1990-95

Saturday, June 13
TEACHING HISTORY AT DEERFIELD ACADEMY — History Department

"As Natural as Breathing"
Thomas A. Heise, Chair, History Department

Images of Deerfield
A Multi-Media Presentation by Grant S. Quasha '98

GRAND CELEBRATION SYMPOSIA — OCTOBER 2-4, 1998

Friday, October 2
The Alumni Program for Our School
THROUGH A LOOKING GLASS BRIGHTLY: PERSPECTIVES ON A CHANGING WORLD

> Moderator: *Frederick D. Barton '67, Director, US AID,*
> *Bureau for Humanitarian Response, Office of Transition Initiatives*
> Responders: *M. Dozier Gardner '51, Vice Chairman and Director, Eaton Vance Corp.*
> *Carrie E. Freeman '92, Analyst, Goldman, Sachs & Co.;*
> *August '98, Senior Analyst, Disney*
> *Warren Zimmermann '52, Kathryn and Shelby Cullom Davis Professor in the Practice of*
> *International Diplomacy, Columbia University;*
> *former Ambassador to Yugoslavia (1989-92)*
> *Dwayne A. Gathers '80, Director of the State of California's Office of Trade and*
> *Investment in Johannesburg, South Africa*
> *Gilbert M. Grosvenor '49, Chairman, National Geographic Society's Board of Trustees*
> *and Education Foundation*
> *Kerry A. Emanuel '73, Professor, Program in Atmospheres, Oceans, and Climate,*
> *Department of Earth, Atmospheric, and Planetary Sciences, M.I.T.*

A MOVING PICTURE: VALUES AND TOLERANCE IN A CHANGING CULTURE

> Moderator: *Stephen G. Smith '67P, Editor "U.S. News & World Report"*
> Panelists: *Robert B. Binswanger '48, Educator*
> *Eliot R. Cutler '64, Law Partner, Cutler & Stanfield*
> *Ferrell P. McClean P'94, '98, Managing Director, J.P. Morgan & Company, Inc.*
> *Elizabeth M. Clement S'66, Minister, First Congregational Church UCC, Atlanta,*
> *Georgia*
> *Steven D. Brill '68, Chairman and CEO, Brill Media Ventures, L.P.;*
> *Founder and Editor-in-Chief, "Brill's Content"*

THE BICENTENNIAL CONVOCATION

> Presenter: *Peter Fallon, Poet, Editor and Publisher*

> Bicentennial Address
> Keynote Speakers:
> *Alice S. Ilchman P'85, President Emerita, Sarah Lawrence College;*
> *Chairman of the Board, Rockefeller Foundation*
> *Warren F. Ilchman P'85, Director, The Paul and Daisy Soros Fellowships for New*
> *Americans*

Saturday, October 3
The School's Program for Our Alumni
REFRACTING THE PAST: RECONSIDERATIONS OF OUR HISTORY

> Moderator: *Brian A. Rosborough '58, Chairman and Founder, Earthwatch Expeditions*
> Panelists: *Thomas G. Clark '67P, Deerfield Apple Farmer*
> *Charles E. Danielski '53, Teacher of Science, Deerfield Academy*
> *Donald R. Friary P'92,'93, Executive Director and Secretary, Historic Deerfield, Inc.*
> *Thomas A. Heise, Chair, History Department, Deerfield Academy*
> *Karinne T. Heise, Teacher of English, Deerfield Academy*

ON DEERFIELD'S HORIZON: EDUCATIONAL VISTAS AHEAD

> Moderator: *Martha C. Lyman, Assistant Head and Director of College Advising*
> Panelists: *Christina B. Rosenberger '98, Undergraduate, Harvard University*
> *Richard A. Bonanno P'91, Dean of the Faculty, Deerfield Academy*
> *Malcolm McKenzie, Principal, Maru a Pula School, Botswana*
> *Suzanne Hannay, Teacher of English, Deerfield; Co-Head (with Eric Widmer)*
> *Bicentennial Educational Initiatives*
> *Ifeoma J. Nwokoye '93, West Africa Program Manager, Africare*

THE TRANSCENDENT MIRROR: OUR SCHOOL AT THE MILLENNIUM

> Moderator: *Robert M. Dewey, Jr. '49, President, Board of Trustees, Deerfield Academy*
> Panelists: *Robert L. Merriam '43P, Used, Rare, and Antique Book Dealer;*
> *Faculty Emeritus, Deerfield Academy*
> *Frank C. Henry, Jr. '69, Chair, English Department; John J. Louis Chair in English,*
> *Deerfield Academy*
> *Meera S. Viswanathan H'95, Associate Professor of Comparative Literature and East*
> *Asian Studies, Brown University; Teacher of English and History, Deerfield Academy*

REFLECTIONS

> Introduction *Bryce V. Lambert, Faculty Emeritus*
> Speaker *Eric Widmer '57, Headmaster*

Sunday, October 4

CELEBRATION WORSHIP SERVICE

> Clergy: *The Reverend Paul W. Buckwalter '52*
> *The Reverend Elizabeth M. Clement S'66 (Arthur J. Clement '66)*

DEERFIELD ACADEMY PRESS

ANDREA MOORHEAD   EDITOR
ROBERT MOORHEAD   DESIGNER
SANDRA LIVELY   EDITORIAL ASSISTANT

§

PRINTED IN THE UNITED STATES OF AMERICA

HULL PRINTING
MERIDEN CONNECTICUT